MW01435456

When Love Works,
When it Doesn't,
When It Settles

WHY DO WE LOVE?

POETRY AND SHORT STORIES
BY AMERICAN WRITERS
EDITORS GLENN PROCTOR AND TRISH STUKBAUER

outskirts
press

Why Do We Love?
When Love Works, When It Doesn't, When It Settles
All Rights Reserved.
Copyright © 2022 Poetry and Short Stories by American Writers / Editors Glenn Proctor and Trish Stukbauer
v2.0

This is a work of poeticized non-fiction. The opinions expressed in this manuscript are solely the opinions of the author and do not represent the opinions or thoughts of the publisher. The author has represented and warranted full ownership and/or legal right to publish all the materials in this book.

This book may not be reproduced, transmitted, or stored in whole or in part by any means, including graphic, electronic, or mechanical without the express written consent of the publisher except in the case of brief quotations embodied in critical articles and reviews.

Outskirts Press, Inc.
http://www.outskirtspress.com

ISBN: 978-1-9772-4437-6

Cover Photo © 2022 Trish Stukbauer. All rights reserved - used with permission.

Outskirts Press and the "OP" logo are trademarks belonging to Outskirts Press, Inc.

PRINTED IN THE UNITED STATES OF AMERICA

Table of Contents

FOREWORD	i
EDITOR'S NOTE	II
WHY DO WE LOVE?	IV
THE WRITERS	vii
LOVE AND LAUGHTER IN FOURS	1
MAHOGANY EYES	2
SIX DECADES	3
GENETIC LUST	4
LOVE'S POTBELLY	5
THE ONE	6
THE VILLAGE	7
LOVE ON THE NILE	8
THE BEST KIND OF LOVE	9
A VISIONARY'S LOVE FOR COMMUNITY	10
CARLTON CORDELL – FIRST KISS (1923-1996)	12
RON (1938-2020)	13
SELF-LOVE	14
MAKING LOVE OR JUST HAVING SEX	15
WHEN A MAN LOVES A WOMAN	16
LET ME COUNT THE WAYS	17
REIGNITE PASSION	18
GRANDMOTHER'S LOVE	19
THRIVING WITH A BROKEN HEART	20
THE BATHROBE	21
TEXAS TOAST AND NARCISSISTIC YOU	22
PENCILS IN MY NOSE	23
SUSTAINS	24
DOVE'S VOICE	25
OLD SOUL	26
PRIMAL	27
LOVE NEVER RUSTS	28
COSMIC COMICS	29
FOUND	31
COSMIC CONSCIOUSNESS	32
LOVE GHOST	33
ALBATROSS	34
MY FIRST REAL KISS	35
HE NEVER LOVED ME!	36

SELF-BETRAYAL...	37
IF LOVE IS... a poem to my future	38
THERE AND NOT THERE	39
QUICK at 3	40
MID-BOOK BREAK	41
TRUE? FALSE?	42
GOOD PARTNER TRAITS	43
FAVORITE (sad and wonderful) LOVE SONGS	45
OMNIPRESENT	46
OH, HOW I LOVE A DAY AT THE BEACH!	47
DEAR DAD	48
REVELATION	49
RESURGENCE	50
UNFOLDING	51
WITHOUT	52
BEYOND THE WORDS	53
ILLUSION	54
THE RED ROOM	55
BLACK BOXES	56
MASTECTOMY	57
BEHIND THE MASK (a short trilogy)	58
BEHIND THE MASK II	59
BEHIND THE MASK III	60
QUESTION?	61
LEFT HISTORY	62
LOVE FALLING, LOVE RISING	63
MORE?	64
NEVER TOGETHER, ALWAYS TOGETHER	65
SEARCH & SURVIVAL & SANITY	66
THAT KINDA' LOVE...	67
THAT KINDA' LOVE	68
THAT KINDA' LOVE	69
WHAT KIND OF A WOMAN?	70
THE CHOICE	72
HE SAID HE LOVED ME...	73
DATING AFTER 50	74
THE COIN TOSS	75
MY OREO	77
MY BEACH WEEK CRUSH	78
LAUNCH	79
ARMOR AND APRON	80

JUST A SWINGIN'	81
AGAPE	82
A PRAYER FOR MY HEART	83
UNPRINTABLE	84
"TO MY GOD-DAMN YANKEE"	85
Red Birds & Roses	86
LONGING	87
WHERE ARE THE MEN?	88
TO LOVE IS DIVINE	89
FATHER, LOVER, UNCLE, BROTHER	90
ELECTRIC LOVE	91
LET'S LOVE LIKE CATS AND DOGS	92
THIS THING CALLED LOVE	93
LETTERS TO SELF	94
BOOKS BY OUR WRITERS (available amazon.com)	98

FOREWORD

Why Do We Love?

To answer this question, we must first ask: What is Love?

It is sharing a quiet evening together, a gift of roses and chocolate, or a passionate evening of lovemaking. Love can be fierce, yet fleeting, or endearing and eternal.

Love takes many forms throughout a day or a lifetime. And, it is all love. The more encompassing your definition of love, the more love you can experience.

Love is a force that brings us together. It connects us to each other at a deeper level. In its purest form, it is unconditional. At the core of our being, we are love.

Love is not only actions; it is a mindset. It means different things to different people and can vary in form from day to day, yet it always starts from within you. It is about feeling, showing and receiving.

It begins with loving yourself and emanates outward because only when you have love in your own heart, can you then share it with others.

So, back to the question: Why Do We Love?

I have been working in the relationship field for more than 35 years. My belief is that being part of a loving, supportive, intimate relationship is one of the best experiences that life has to offer. Read more of Lori's thoughts on love and relationships in the following pages.

Our overall happiness, physical health and our longevity are significantly influenced by the quality of our relationships. As humans, we are biologically wired to seek connections with others. We have a fundamental desire to feel needed, loved and cared for.

Whether it is the fire fueled by a passionate kiss or baring our soul to another, we desire to feel love, be loved and share love.

Lori Ann Davis, MA, CRS
Author, Coach & Certified Relationship Specialist

EDITOR'S NOTE

Writing about Love, Lust, Affection and Relationships is scary. But very doable...

Gather together a bunch of recovering journalists, several authors and new writers and challenge them to write about what is probably the most written about, worried about, talked about, dramatized and enjoyed subject in history.

This book looks at the divergent aspects of relationships and gets to the heart of our humanity and who we are as individuals. For all of us, writing about love was a mental and emotional challenge: a blessing, a curse, a conflict, a pleasure, a pain, a passion...

How do we define love? What are its risks and rewards? Can a broken heart ever mend? Who or what do we love? Spouse? Partner? Family? Friends? Pets? Country? Or, do we love shiny objects, what we have or what we have done?

What is love to each of us? Is it joy, marriage, living together, 50-year relationships, lustful one-nighters and long weekends, or a warm body to ward off loneliness? How often do we settle in place because of children, money, lifestyle and familiarity?

In 2020 and 2021, how has the pandemic affected our relationships?

This is the second book project by **WRITINGBOOTCAMP/Charlotte**, a 6-month creative writing program I founded in 2016. For this project, we included other writers from Charlotte and a few journalism friends from around the country.

Our first book - with 13 writers - ***CHANGE, CREATIVITY, CURIOSITY AND HOPE IN A CRISIS CALLED PANDEMIC*** *- was* published in November 2020. It was co-edited by recovering journalist and marketing consultant Trish Stukbauer, who also designed this cover and used an old Kent State blue pen for final editing on this manuscript.

This book is not a psychological analysis, but a "gut-level" look at love, affection and relationships, and the decisions, good and bad, made by the writers. Some pieces are extremely raw and revealing, others positive and tender love stories. We can gain hope, however, from the Foreword, written by relationship specialist Lori Ann Davis, a nationally recognized coach who has written or collaborated on seven books about relationships.

Readers will, most likely, see themselves, past relationships or relate to some of the experiences written about in this book. During the creation of this manuscript, several writers said they were asked about their pieces for the book or the book's topic.

My response: As adults, all of us have a past, years of baggage and have, most likely, dealt with favorable and unfavorable relationship situations. Love – or the appearance of love and affection – is fragile, misunderstood and imperfect, yet still very real. As Mandy Hale wrote, "If it's not making you better, it isn't love. True love makes you more of who you are, not less."

Thank you for reading. Enjoy good relationships!
Glenn Proctor

WHY DO WE LOVE?

Attraction, Affection, Attention, Comfort, Fear, Lust, Opportunity, Trust...

Glenn Proctor

'Tis often the best and worst of life, this thing that makes people sing, cling, give a ring, take a ring, travel far, slam doors, open doors, flirt, fake, smile, frown, forgive, forget, understand, misunderstand, respect, disrespect, run to, run from, dress, undress, moan, penetrate, cry, *laugh*, offend, defend, mend, write, fight, feel, act real, separate and ask why, when, where and how it happens?

Never a paved road or superhighway, but a worn path, love's an ocean of bound experiences, a crystal chalice filled with sand from two sets of feet after a midnight beach walk and a solemn kiss under moon's spotlight.

Love is that dogwood blossom, one morning glory at early light, a smile that widens as that face appears, that sun at mid-day, a search for evening serenity, that feeling as cold hands clutch and warm, a long journey, a quickie, a not-so-long episode neither wrong or out of place – just good.

When we find love, then what? What if it whisks us into feelings never felt, passion never imagined and words never heard? What do we do? Can we run with fear? Or, should we allow love to devour us with new pleasure?

When is the right time for love? Does love often come and go like the seasons, causing the best and worst of emotions? Must we prepare for love?

Attraction is a surprise - that note, that text, that poem, that flower for no reason other than to toss a flare into one's heart, make one's day brighter or connecting to look into one's eyes, asking for a small piece of one's soul.

Attraction, infatuation, affection, like, love and lust – feelings that exceed our normality and speed our thinking when we're alone. Can you join an unexpected journey because it feels so right?

Love is children, parents, family, friends and those you love even more, near or far. Love can be a surprising mix, a blending of colors, ethnicities, preferences, religions and ages to form a relationship, a family...

Love is broken hearts and dark clouds finding new sun called romance, a pair of hearts curious, pushing against the fear that new brings, fighting torrential doubt and outside rain, finding time to meld aspirations, getting to know and understand, when infatuation turns to love. Love is an invisible mask.

Real love is not arrogant or one-sided, a game for blame, one expecting all and giving less. Love is a patient soul, yet often a tortured soul. Love is without supremacy. Yet, we often love when the other doesn't love back.

Love can be risky - how risky depends on those involved. It's a distant star coming close, coming to satisfy a heart for a period, mind and body disappearing into life's abyss after experiences, bold and exciting. Often, experiences happen, surprising, unexplained... Not forever, just for a season... life, affection and love have so many chapters...

What is forever love? Is destiny more than one love, opportunities that blossom from a solemn kiss, a flirt that flourishes, a hug that feels whole and never-ending? Love, with its charm and nuances, haunts, whispers and endears often without explanation. Love forever or love for a time...

Love is mind exploration, knowing the best and worst of another, a search to understand experiences, moods, habits, days and curiosity. Though, years of love never reveal all. Do we ever really know the all of another?

Love is exploration, bodies woven into motion so pleasurable that it cries with intense joy. When lips, tongues, hands, arms, legs, breasts explore and tangle in ecstasy, 'tis the best. When love comes, when affection is priority, give as much body as you give mind. Bodies then explode with bliss.

Is there love at first sight as history says? Is there attraction/infatuation after brief non-physical interludes, two finding comfort in shared conversation and an occasional flirt that beckons for more? If life is reality, can a short run to new arms, with lightning kisses, be satisfying without emotional discomfort? Can one love more than one? Can two show torrid affection before fleeing?

Love is silly, a playground, two on the swings, up and down on a sliding board, a picnic on grass, a race to get out of the rain, a water gun fight, a passionate shower, a beach, favorite songs, a pillow fight, rushed affection.

Love is healthy, is supportive, is special, is a celebration, is something to cheer for... When it's right, it's amazing, a decision of life, serenity's best.

Love understands the misunderstandings that appear on bad days, love is that meal that satisfies, sleeping naked, that movie or show causing tears or laughter, that warm feeling when one is away and safe. Love sprints, then slows, talks softly, gets agitated, cools and laughs. Love stifles, overwhelming naïve souls desiring more than infatuation. Love settles, gives in because departing is too great a burden.

New love is scary and exciting because curiosity is a mental commodity. To get love is to give love, to speak is also to listen, to be at peace with oneself is to be ready for love, to accept love, to sustain and nurture love.

Infatuation can be uncomfortable, not knowing for certain, wondering if initial thoughts aren't real or imagined, a touch or look, a reaction to feelings or nothing at all. Infatuation is a dusty road, a path littered with thorns, a super highway into the unknown where rejections often lie.

Is infatuation early love, yet closer to the mind than the heart, with its own reality? Is infatuation a reach for invisible air, a blueprint for life's expansion, that feeling that prompts questions?

Who is that person and why do I care? What if they dismiss me? What if they surprise me and want a relationship? Am I ready?

Love is often not sharing the same space, same meals or same air. Yet, it feels intense, woven deep in our souls. Love is a ring, then it's not. Love is actions and words, then it's not. Love is sex, then it's not. Love is curious. Love is amazing, then, it's not. Or, love is amazing and sustaining.

Love is many conversations, the short ones, the long ones, the ones with laughter, the ones with tears, dreams revealed, thoughts revealed... when subtle information and history is passed and understood.

Despite its hazards and hesitations, infatuation, then love, are opportunities — new chances to live, to breathe, to blend, to extinguish drama, to find laughter, have logical conversations, to be understood, to be proud.

Love is the talk that helps hearts find truce, brings voices to apologies, finds hearts and minds reaching for strength for days ahead and more years. Love, when mature, finishes sentences without surprise, feels mood changes and works to put an out-of-sync partner back together.

Love is intelligent, knows that special day when it feels right, when finding that place where harmony and serenity live, when hearts are alive with hope. Love is an experience worth having, a real adventure.

But keep this caution in mind from Irish poet and playwright Oscar Wilde

"Never love anyone who treats you like you're ordinary."

THE WRITERS

Lizz Baxter - An Army veteran of Operation Iraqi Freedom in 2002, she comes from a small Nebraska railroad town. Writing from a young age through the encouragement of her grandmother, Lizz tells stories of her adventures around the world and as a young female soldier. Arriving in Charlotte in 2012, she serves the community and fellow veterans as a real estate broker. When she is not working with clients, she is shooting and editing video footage, attempting yoga handstands, roller skating, exploring Charlotte's secret places, supporting local businesses, or out for long walks and bike rides with her husband, Monte.

Ty Burton – A native of West Chester, PA, Ty is the author of *A Journey to Manhood, The Village that Raised the Boy*. A former college basketball player, now a corporate strategy & change execution advisor, he has written for industry publications, including the Change Management Review, Talent Management Magazine and Accenture Outlook Journal, where he writes about the intersection of leadership and business transformation. Serena is Ty and Miesha's daughter, a writing eight-year-old.

Toni Cordell – Born in San Francisco, graduating from high school reading at the 5th grade level, unable to spell, Toni felt cheated of opportunity. She admits to being academically slow, suggesting she is like a snail on Valium, but is always moving forward. As a cinematographer, she shot 16mm film documentaries in Kenya, India and Central America. She interviewed Mother Theresa and an Alabama Death Row inmate. The author of a dog book highlighting diversity, she is a graduate of Central Piedmont Community College and hopes to return to her studies at Queens University.

Lori Ann Davis - A therapist, coach and relationship specialist for more than 35 years, Lori's mission is "helping singles and couples create the relationship of their dreams." A former coach on the nationwide Radical Dating Documentary Show, she is the author of *Unmasking Secrets to Unstoppable Relationships, 365 Ways to Ignite Her Love, A Couples Love Journal and Love Habits*. She has contributed to other relationship books.

Doreen Day - Doreen admits that her discovery of writing is a recent endeavor that has become a passion. An avid reader, her goal is to create provocative work through inspired thought and exceptional research. Saying her work comes from life experience and exquisite detail, her creativity extends to stained glass and drawing. A former partner in a title insurance company for 25 years, Doreen has a deep affinity for animals, especially greyhounds that she has rescued and rehabilitated for three decades. A massage therapist and Reiki Master- practitioner, the Catskills Mountains of New York native resides in Western North Carolina.

Jeff Ferebee- A former member of the 82nd Airborne Division, he graduated from West Point with a Bachelor of Science degree in literature. Jeff deployed in support of Operation Inherent Resolve as a platoon leader in 2015. He stays connected to the veteran community, grows vegetables, and practices the healing nature of art on Sugar Mountain Farms, outside Nashville, TN, while cherishing time with family.

Alice Flowers – Owner of AF Image Group LLC, a boutique-style image consulting firm, Alice moved from Minnesota to Charlotte to be closer to family and became a fulltime entrepreneur after leaving corporate life. A former young model and fashion show producer, she has had years of self-doubt and personal insecurities and incorporates her own style of mental toughness into her career-building and image workshops. When she is not writing, she is putting together plans for her business and working as a Mary Kay sales consultant.

John Masson - John Masson is a pen name for a former journalist who worked at small weekly newspapers in Louisiana and Mississippi for more than two decades. A University of Mississippi graduate, he also spent time in the Peace Corps. John now lives on a houseboat on the Finger Lakes in upstate New York.

Lori Myers – Lori's love of books began as a child. One of her first literary loves was *"Harold and the Purple Crayon"* by Crocket Johnson. Through Harold's adventures Lori believed then (and still does today) that all things are possible! Lori is innately curious and self-reflective by nature. Combine this with her love for family, faith, history, and the power of words, she's inspired to write stories and poems that reflect all her loves. In 2021, Lori published her first solo work, *Glimpses of Tenderness: Soothing the Soul Through Reminiscence*. Outside her career in information technology, Lori is a life coach who focuses on helping others discover their potential by exploring possibilities.

Marisa Porto – An assistant dean at the Scripps Howard School of Journalism and Communications at Hampton University in Virginia,

Marisa also teaches management and entrepreneurship courses. Prior to joining the university, she led business and news operations at Tribune Publishing's Virginia Media. An alumnus of the University of South Carolina, Marisa is on the news advisory council for the Trust Project, past president of the Virginia Press Association and served on Virginia's Freedom of Information Advisory Council. Her children are three loving collies.

Glenn "Jarhead Poet" **Proctor** – Founder, ***WRITINGBOOTCAMP/ Charlotte***; author of five books, executive coach, mental health and suicide prevention educator, grief coach, media professor, 40 year-journalist, Pulitzer Prize winner, Pulitzer Prize judge, Marine gunnery sergeant and Vietnam veteran. Glenn, who retired as vice president and executive editor of the Richmond Times-Dispatch and created *REDDjobb Coaching*, writes poetry and coaches from lived experience: foster kid, single parent and alcoholic. A victim of Agent Orange poisoning, he is a prostate cancer survivor.

Beryl Rayford - A mental health enthusiast who fully realizes how taking care of our minds drastically improves how we live, Beryl is a Certified Peer Support Specialist and trained Mental Health Storyteller. Her training fuels her focus to reduce mental health stigma and create a connection with others on their life journeys.

Kimberly Shelton – A native Texan & former military brat now residing in Charlotte, NC. She's a fun-loving, dance-until-you-drop kind of gal. She adores all things animal & is a parent to those with paws. Reading, writing, dancing & yoga captivate her interest. She's enchanted with Motown, R&B, soul, funk & jazz. She's a wanna-be mosaic artist. She resonates with the raw & emotional, so whenever you read her writing, a piece of her heart remains with you always.

Elizabeth "Libby" Smoot – Libby loves Jesus, her family and the Pittsburgh Steelers. When she isn't reading, writing and learning, she enjoys traveling with her husband and sharing in the lives of their three adult children. She does most of this from her home in the northern Shenandoah Valley of Virginia. Libby, who spent 28 years in journalism, is now working in marketing and communications for Virginia-based Trex Company.

Trish Stukbauer – An author, recovering journalist, and multi-platform communications professional, Trish is editor of *Showtime Car Culture*, and director of communications for Holy Comforter Church in Charlotte. As owner of i.e. marketing, she works with clients ranging from an international business incubator and globally recognized home décor retailer to advertising agencies on both coasts, non-profit organizations (CNE, CDE, CNC), businesses, authors and celebrities. In her previous life, she was a newspaper and home magazine editor.

Diane Weekley - Board Certified Coach and long-time storyteller, Diane believes in the power of myth and story to shape lives. With a focus on empowering others to discover and live their truth, Diane coaches individuals and couples to restore and strengthen significant relationships. Diane works as a network director with Charlotte-based Veterans Bridge Home to support veterans and military families transition successfully to civilian life. In her leisure time, she enjoys writing, reading fantasy fiction, and exploring life with family and grandchildren.

LOVE AND LAUGHTER IN FOURS

(what happens when writers think too much...)

If I was your lover
And you kissed me goodbye
I'd find a big hand fan
To keep my face dry...

If I was an apple
And you were a peach
I'd build a new shelf
To keep both in reach.

If you were an old phone
And I was the ringer
I'd find the right love song
And be the best singer.

If you were a rainbow
And I was the view
I'd search all the colors
Until I found you...

In future conversations
When we talk about sex
Stay normal and natural
Not so darn complex.

Love is amazing
Love is a rule.
Love all you can
But don't be a fool.
Love can be sexy
Love can be blind
Love can be painful.
Love can be kind.

MAHOGANY EYES

Lizz Baxter

Lost in your Mahogany Eyes
Time eludes me
Incapable of escape
I'm Captivated!

Your eyes say
Deeply Connected
I wonder if mine say
Unhinged.

Our time has not arrived
This moment must last forever
No words, no Judgment
Pure Understanding.

We belong together
Yet separated by circumstance
In this moment, all I need
Is to be seen by your Mahogany Eyes.

SIX DECADES

Lizz Baxter

Grandma's delicate fingers shuffle papers into taller piles. Today, we will sort through six decades of memories printed on yellowed paper.

"Oh..." she sighs. "I make a horrible widow." I pick up an overdue bill to fan away my tears. I can't look at into her sad blue eyes today. It's time to be strong.

I am here to scrub carpet and clear a pathway through her irreplaceable boxes of memories.

Grandpa gave up years ago on this project, but he is gone now. We lost our family patriarch yesterday. It was his birthday. I was honored to share the full cycle of life. No suffering, just old age. A desirable outcome after a long life lived. He was a musical man that sang until his last breath.

Grandma trusts me. I'm her oldest granddaughter. She knows I won't question her. We read aloud, laugh and drink tea while she tells me what we will keep. I ask her to retrieve another memory from the back room so I can manage to sneak a few unsalvageable pieces into the bin.

Grandma is 90 years old herself, so who am I to tell her what she can keep? I continue gazing at her old letters from near and far.

Eventually, Grandma shuffles around the corner, returning to our project with her head down, staring into her hands. She smiles to herself softly as she hands me a framed black and white photo. My favorite of young newlyweds taken from the front seat to the back. A small portion of the bench seat blurring out the bottom left corner.

Two young faces I've never seen apart. Two voices that harmonized on separate phones of the same landline to "Happy Birthday" and "We Wish You a Merry Christmas." Sixty years of life together and finishing each other's sentences.

I look up from the photo. We stand together in silence.

Our eyes meet and she whispers, "We were very much in Love."

GENETIC LUST

Lizz Baxter

Years of infidelity are passed down like
Tarnished heirlooms embedded in bloodlines
Fantasy flipping reality upside down like
Overturned dinner tables and broken china...

A perfect recipe for the emotionally lonely
Attention starved with a swirl of booze
Sultry smiles and gazes lock in
Raised highball glasses chime up high...

Like being seen for the first time again
Heads tilt back in pleasure and laughter
Emboldened by avoiding a close call
Ice melting as the heat rises, blood boils and our minds race...

Inhibitions low as fingers draw love notes on napkins
Suppression of entangled emotion
Brushes with exposure bring more excitement
While hidden in dark shadows and backseats.

LOVE'S POTBELLY

Lizz Baxter

Love is sexy. Sexy is skinny. No jiggles. Suck in those thighs. Work harder. Run longer. Eat less. Stand taller until your rejected curves ache. You will be good enough one day.

Love was lost. She needed an extended vacation from a culture that rejected her. Exhausted from her daily pursuit of self worth. Tired of counting calories on fingers and toes. Report to the scale promptly every A.M. and P.M. Futile attempts to eliminate sustenance today, by nibbling at nothing until tomorrow. Eat this, not that. Split "halvsies." The calorie chart says no. Read the label. Contains sugar. 'Put it back' roars her neglected belly.

Love is Fat. Fat is Unworthy. Hide from the mirror. Don't let your sex appeal flatten like flabby ass cheeks. You should be ashamed.

Love decided enough was enough. It was time she found a place where she belonged. A place that celebrated her curves. She longed to be free. To indulge. To live a little. She dug deep inside her soul to discover she was more than her overworked muscles.

Love's mind needed some squats and curls. She needed support from a new culture. She longed to be embraced and accepted so she could shift her mindset. Her stay extended from months to years. There was no turning back; life had led her in a different direction. Away from the familiar into a new state of mind.

Tight tummy spilled over jean's waistband. Defined muscles turned soft. Comfort food replaced veggies. Curves expanded. At first, she feared rejection. Yet, she had never felt so whole.

Love was never fat and certainly not unworthy. Others needed her, wanted to know her, celebrated her curves. She saw herself with new eyes. Embraced, accepted and whole. She did not need to hide from the mirror. She just needed to see her true self. She gave herself to others and they back to her.
She did the work. Bodies can change. Acceptance of self was the peace she needed.

Love was never lost. Just misplaced.

THE ONE

Lizz Baxter

It's 5 a.m. We've been up all night. The morning sunrise glows in the window. The microwave clock must need resetting. We blink at each other in disbelief. We have been talking for hours. Yet, there is still so much to say.

I sit in my perch on the countertop. You lean against the dishwasher. It's winter. I'm wearing your hoodie over my club clothes.

"It was too damn cold to wear this outfit anyway," I say. You laugh and look down and away. We are in the kitchen sharing life stories. Our conversations shift from lighthearted to deep and back again.

You came to my rescue. The girls thought I needed to be out. "Shop the market," they said. My divorce is finalized. You were up thinking anyway. Your mother just started chemo. I cry on your shoulder. In your own way, you cry on mine, too.

I know it seems soon. We haven't known each other long, but I can't imagine a future without you. Right now, I'm unsure in what capacity. We are best friends. We are others. We are outsiders. We are dreamers. We are connected.

You listen. No fixing. When I ask, you hand me some super glue to patch the broken pieces of myself. No judgment. Just the support I need. I see you. I help you dig into your deepest emotions. You tell me how you really feel. I translate even more. Your eyes tell me all your fears, your pain and worry.

I assure you that we are lucky. You believe me. Together, we carefully navigate life's setbacks. We try our best to make sense and ponder the fairness of it all. We approach each other honestly. We let our guards down. Set aside the bullshit. That's what friends are for.

Right now, it's time for coffee. It's one of our favorite pastimes. We have shared an awful cup or two in the cafeteria and a few at the local Dunkin'. Today, let's be fancy. It's Saturday, "Let's go to Central Coffee," we say with a laugh.

We enter into the coffee shop in a daze from a sleepless night and our newly intertwined worlds. We stand quietly together in line uninterrupted by the buzz. A moment or two passes and the barista shouts sarcastically from behind the bar.

"Can you two stop being 'so in love' and order. You're next in line..."

We look at each other once again in disbelief. Could you be the one?

THE VILLAGE

Ty Burton

Born to a teenage mother, my father's involvement in my life lasted as long as this sentence. So early on, I learned to fully appreciate my mother's determination, harnessing her inner turmoil and demons from childhood to provide a better life for us.

I never wanted for anything. My mother's love was my sustenance. Throughout my early years, I rarely thought about not having a father. Maybe, it was because not having a father seemed to be commonplace among my friends.

My mother is a brilliant, unflappable woman. Despite giving birth to me in her junior year of high school, she graduated a year later with a 3.2 grade point average. Never one to be deterred, she earned a four-year degree at age 50, while serving as the family psychologist, banker and landlord to all throughout the years.

Some of my favorite childhood moments were spent with my aunts and uncles at my grandmother's house, throwing the football around in the backyard, trips to Virginia Beach or simply visiting friends. My grandmother's house was always vibrant with the sounds of soul music, hip hop, sibling rivalry, thrown objects and, most of all, Love.

My village extends beyond family and includes teachers, coaches, mentors and extended family friends. Because of them, I learned the importance of perseverance, determination and the transformative power of education and athletics.

Through the years, I've found the true power of the village has been the enduring nature of those lessons, transcending generations, as my wife and I impart them on our young daughter, Serena.

Thank God for the power and love of the village.

LOVE ON THE NILE

Ty Burton

She's the queen of the Nile River Valley,
The depths of her beauty greater than the mouth
of the mighty Mediterranean.
You see this warrior princess was sweeter than
sugar cane in times dated pre-colonial.
Excuse me, sister, what tribe do you come from?
Asante, Dahomey, Shabazz?
You know, the lost tribe.
Can I be your African scribe?
Take you on a freedom ride.
I became her Sun; she became my Earth,
A love so righteous and divine...
On the Nile River Valley,
There's the beauty of Black love.

THE BEST KIND OF LOVE

Serena & Ty Burton

Family love is the best kind of love,
It hugs you in a warm grandmotherly embrace,
It's my eight-year-old daughter, Serena
Being cheered on by family during her first dance recital
Letting her know that we are in this place.

Family love is the best kind of love
A Valentine's Day with no end;
Like meeting my wife for the first time all over again.

Family love is the best kind of love,
It's writing this poem with my daughter
From beginning to end,
Showing her how to ride a bike
Falling down… and getting back up again.

A VISIONARY'S LOVE FOR COMMUNITY

Ty Burton

Throughout the early years of my life, many of the lifelong friendships and character-building experiences that shaped me as an adult were borne out of the vision of one man, Dr. Leslie Pickney Hill. His love for community led to the founding of a community center in my hometown, West Chester, PA.

Dr. Hill envisioned a community-based institution that would help address the unmet needs of the local black community. The guiding principles of his vision were to foster and promote a greater understanding and cooperation between all citizens through education.

In August 1918, Dr. Hill's vision came to fruition and the community center was born.

The "Center" has been a treasure and stronghold for countless years in the black community. My grandmother, now in her 80s, actually attended kindergarten there, and my mother worked there for a short period when I was in diapers.

My late grandfather also had a community center story, replacing his twin brother in a basketball lineup to face off against a Wilt Chamberlain-led team, where my grandfather scored 50 points.

For my friends and me, the center was our savior and kept us out of trouble. The place instilled a sense of confidence and pride in how I saw myself in relation to the rest of society. The center director was black, as were the staff, the program administrators, camp counselors and grounds crew – this during a time when I was often the only black kid in my school classes.

As kids, we spent our summer months at the pool and on the basketball court. Those courts (both inside and outside) often drew some of the best area players, including many local trash talkers and high school stars who later played college ball.

I hear the editor of this book played a lot at the center against some well-known regional players (Jimmy Bell, George Bratcher, Fred Sadler, Leon Bell (my middle school basketball coach), Bobby Dorsey, Mike Gallimore and Andy Toth, to name a few).

Above all, the center was a place for community, hosting talent shows, teen parties, holiday events and neighborhood festivals and housed a number of early childhood education and tutoring programs.

It was also a place that honored hard work and stressed education as a way to success. Throughout the years, the center played a role in producing countless students who received undergraduate, graduate, doctorate and law degrees.

The center was a true testimony to Dr. Hill's vision, leadership and love of community.

CARLTON CORDELL – FIRST KISS (1923-1996)

Toni Cordell

Life needed a change. I had done some very minor modeling. At 5-foot, 2 inches, Vogue magazine was not coming for me. The agency I was signed with suggested that I was animated enough to consider film work.

Even though no proper profile photo sheet was available, I took a day to drive to San Francisco - the City by the Bay, about an hour from home in Danville, California. Just interested in what the possibility might be.

In the crowded waiting room, a slender attractive older blond man was flirting with all the female hopefuls. I did not reciprocate. After my time behind a closed-door conversation, I left. Going down two flights of worn wooden steps, I don't know why I suspected that man would follow me.

As I turned to leave the building, I slowed up on the street and, sure enough, I heard him call out. I acted like I didn't hear him. So, he hurried and caught up.

"May I buy you a drink?"

With my smart-alecky attitude, I crowed, "I don't drink."

"May I buy you a cup of coffee?" He responded.

Still snooty, "I don't drink coffee either."

"Okay, what will it take to sit down and talk with you?" He almost barked at me.

"I'll have a Coke."

We talked for an hour, maybe more. Carlton Cordell, sports announcer/feature reporter for KTVU-TV in Oakland, CA introduced himself to me as I had not seen him on the air. Maybe to impress me, he invited me to follow him across the Bay Bridge to give me a tour of the television station.

Since I was in my own car, it sounded relatively safe. Mr. Cordell gave me a tour and walked me out of the building. It was raining softly.

This man, the flirt that I only met a few hours before placed his strong flat hand at the small of my back. He drew me in, flush body-to-body contact, adding a warm gentle kiss.

For 30-years before his death in 1996, when my husband, Carlton Cordell, placed his hand at the small of my back, I was his.

RON (1938-2020)

Toni Cordell

When my longtime family friend, Ron Meyer, said he would be in Charlotte in August, I presumed he was coming for a conference or meeting.

I suggested he could stay in my downstairs bedroom, with a bathroom. He would have his own private space to feel relaxed and comfortable.

Ron arrived on August 3, 2015. I was delighted to see him and excited that we might have time for a visit. He had always been fun, and I enjoyed his company.

Within 10 minutes of being in the house and just sitting down, Ron asked, "Would you be open to marrying me?"

"Are you serious?" I stared at him.

"Yes."

I then pointed north. "Rockford!"

"No. Charlotte," he said.

Strangely enough, I guess I never answered Ron because he thought I said, "No." But I didn't. Somehow, I was able to divert the conversation elsewhere. Thank God.

Friends for 40 years, but I had no idea Ron thought about me that way.

Would I love him? Was I attracted to him? Well, I already loved him at some level. But marriage?

We went to dinner, came back for a swim and hours of conversation with laughter until I confessed, "I am tired and have to go to sleep." We went to our assigned rooms.

In the morning, I heard him up and around. We had more conversation, off to breakfast and back to the house.

As Ron was getting ready to leave, he turned to kissed me good-bye. Lip to lip. How strange. We were awkward and didn't fit together naturally. Yet, I wanted more.

Several days later, I said, "Yes." to his proposal.

I also suggested that we would have to practice to get our lips to fit better. Ron had a scar on his mouth from an automobile accident years before. We would work around that even if we needed a tutorial.

Practice, practice, practice...

SELF-LOVE

Toni Cordell

The word Love in the English language can mean, "I love chocolate" or it can mean, "I love a family member" - "a friend" or be about a "mate or lover."

In evaluating the thought of Self-Love, I am trying to figure out if there is a line between self-preservation and arrogance. Would arrogance know when it is ignorant?

Since I grew up without an ounce of confidence, I am not concerned that I would be arrogant. Because I am on a first name basis with failure, that is no threat. I have the courage to plow through until I learn what my current needs are.

And, I am okay because I don't expect to be the smartest person in the room, and being invisible is okay with me. Well, that is, until I have something to say. Then, I will find an opening and mouth my thoughts.

In order to not slide into arrogance, I believe self-examination may be the secret to the proper level of self-love. The Bible teaches us to love our neighbor as ourselves. So, my God has not told me to give out until I am gone. He has told me to value self because HE does.

So, I do. I have thoughts and boundaries and have learned to use my voice.

Self-love in the proper portion reveals itself in the way I/we respect and value each other.

MAKING LOVE OR JUST HAVING SEX

Toni Cordell

As a woman, I hope men can hear my heart. Yes, just having sex has it place. Sometimes that is all there is time for – a sex romp. Trust me, I know there is pleasure far beyond that.

For me, it requires a bit of time and thought. In a covenant marriage, knowing my husband, Ron Meyer, is committed to me as protector and provider, it is very easy to make sure his testosterone levels are appreciated and cared for.

We were married for only a few years, both having been widowed and now in our 70s. While it started 40 years ago in friendship, it took an unexpected visit to the altar for us to become man and wife.

God's plans are remarkable as He developed the male and female architecture for a "One Flesh Union." As humans, we are physical, heart and mind creatures.

I wasn't there when God designed humans, but I would bet that HE Intended the physical joining to be pleasure for both. That requires "making love." Not just having sex.

After our vows, on our wedding night (yes, we waited), Ron asked for the lights to remain on. At my age, I never expected anyone to see this mature body.

"Are you sure? Do you know this body has been around for decades? Also, I have given birth three times."

Ron was ready for our bodies to consummate the vows. Anticipating the journey of joy captured my heart and mind in complete surrender. There was no wonder after the adventure of investigating the peaks and valleys of the physical terrain. Every thrust and reset brings him closer to the precious grin.

Explosion revealed on his face as that satisfied smile stared back at me. Surrendering all to the other while our bodies joined in mutual dance. His beautiful sparking blue eyes nearly closed from exhaustion.

God ordained our marriage. Have at it, enjoy every aspect of it, whether it's just sex or taking time to make love.

Crystals of Rainbow Love ring from the depths of this committed relationship.

WHEN A MAN LOVES A WOMAN

Toni Cordell

She will melt into his arms
    surrender her heart, mind, body and soul
    grow into the person she was designed to be
    in character and femininity
    Shine and Serve... Walk the extra mile...
    choose to know his body as he knows hers
    respond to the desire of his touch

want to overcome her own flaws
    rather than point out his...

When a man loves a woman...
    peace fill the house
    in mutual love and respect
    where all can grow
there is no deception between them
    emotions are clear
    motives are stated
    and naked in their bodies
She is his reward for his devotion and respect...

LET ME COUNT THE WAYS

Lori Ann Davis

When we first met, you seemed perfect, without flaws. Even when I noticed imperfections, I overlooked them and made excuses for them. My body was energized with those feel-good hormones of new love and I had a vested interest in wanting you to be perfect. My secret hope is that when I find my perfect partner, I will finally feel complete.

As time passed, you became less perfect and I was disheartened. Where did my illusion of perfection go? After all, perfection is always an illusion that is unsustainable. I know this and yet, with each new relationship, I hope to find the perfection I crave.

So now, I begin to complain or criticize, which can lead to arguments and hurt feelings. In reality, you haven't changed. My perception of you has changed.

In my 35 years as a therapist, counselor and coach, I have seen this story play out over and over again with couples. It is time to break free of this insanity, so we can experience true love, not the illusion of love.

The key to happiness is radical acceptance of the other person for who they are, flaws and all. This also means releasing the idea that one person or one relationship can make us happy. That is an inside job, whether we like it or not. When we begin to accept each other as a perfectly imperfect person, your relationships can evolve into one of deep passionate love.

Learn to accept others for who they are, quirks and all. See and love them as a whole person. This doesn't mean you have to like everything about them, but you allow them to be who they are. Isn't that what you are hoping for in return?

Why do we expect others to be perfect while we get to be our genuine imperfect selves?

Work on giving respect, expecting respect in return and watch what happens. Your relationship will flourish!

REIGNITE PASSION

Lori Ann Davis

"See there's this place in me where your fingertips still rest, your kisses still linger, and your whispers softly echo. It's the place where a part of you will forever be part of me." Gretchen Kemp

Couples who make passion a priority are more patient, appreciative and forgiving of each other. When a relationship is new, there is usually a great deal of physical touch. We love spending time gazing into each other's eyes, kissing, touching and enjoy each other's company, physically and emotionally. The hormones are going crazy and it feels fantastic!

As a relationship progresses, it's important to maintain physical intimacy. This is not what usually happens. We get busy and forget how much fun it is to linger in bed, enjoying each other's touch. We start saying No to the other person's advances. The hormones subside and we aren't proactive in keeping them alive.

Who has time for sex and pleasure? You do – if you want to keep your relationship alive and passionate! After all, intimacy is what defines a relationship as "intimate" – rather than just a friendship.

It is important to set aside time for intimacy. It doesn't happen without individual effort, but it is worth it. Do something every day. Say Yes instead of No. Get started and see where the experience takes you. Kiss deeper and longer. Flirt with each other like you did when you first started dating.

Just in case you needed more reasons to enjoy sex with your loved one, check this out: the hormones released during physical intimacy – oxytocin, serotonin and dopamine – help us feel safe, cared for and bonded to each other. Physical touch relieves stress and anxiety, improves our immune systems and stokes the desire for more physical connection.

And, sex is fun!

GRANDMOTHER'S LOVE

Lori Ann Davis

Some families eat to live and some live to eat. My family definitely fell into the latter category. Food was not just something that sustained our bodies, it sustained our family unit and nourished our souls.

I was blessed to have spent most of my childhood with my grandparents. My grandmother, Granny, was not only a phenomenal cook, but one of the kindest, most loving women I have ever met. She showed me what true love is all about. My grandparents were living examples of what is possible in life and love. The time spent with them shaped my future relationships and fueled my passion as a therapist and coach. I do my best to carry on this tradition of unconditional love I experienced in my grandparents' home with my three daughters.

When I think of my grandmother, I see her in the kitchen pouring love into whatever fabulous smelling meal she was cooking. I was born and raised in New Orleans by Italian grandparents, so there was always something amazing on the stove. Those are memories of pure love!

My fondest memories as a child are sitting around the kitchen table sharing time together as a family, sometimes for hours. I never tired of this bonding experience; no one ever rushed away from the table to do something else. We lingered enjoying each other's company, listening to stories and sharing ideas. Food was the glue that held our loving family together.

My children and I have created our own routines. Unfortunately, I am unable to share meals with my grandparents, but the traditions live on. Now that my daughters are old enough to help with the cooking, we look forward to discussing meal plans, cooking together, setting the table with grandmother's china and crystal and enjoying a meal together.

The meal is more than just good food; it is a bonding experience that I hope will be with us for the rest of my life and carried on by my children – sharing the love that began with my Grandmother.

THRIVING WITH A BROKEN HEART

Lori Ann Davis

I met my ex-husband when I was 22. It was love at first sight. In reality, it was probably lust at first sight that grew into love. We had a love affair that lasted 25 years. I looked forward to seeing him at the end of every day and getting butterflies in my stomach when he walked in the door. He was the most important thing in my life, and I adored him.

Does that mean we had an easy life with no struggles? Of course not! We had our share of tragedies and difficulties over the years, but through it all, he remained the love of my life.

Eventually, we made the unthinkable decision to part ways, not because we stopped loving each other, but because we both had lessons to learn and things to do that we could not do together.

Not all relationships are meant to last forever. Sometimes, the best path is to part ways.

I remember the first time this thought crossed my mind. I thought I had lost my mind! A life without my husband was unthinkable! Separating was devastating for me because it meant losing my best friend of 25 years and the relationship I thought would last forever. I was not sure how to carry on. It was the hardest thing I have ever had to face and there were times I contemplated not facing life without him.

But my three children needed me and I loved them as much as I loved him. So, I picked myself up and discovered that you can live life with a heart that is shattered in a million pieces.

I knew love would never feel the same again, but I knew I wanted to love again. Not the same love, but a new love. Eventually, I pieced my life back together one minute at a time, one day at a time and moved forward.

I now have a stronger love for myself along with a new man in my life. It is not the same all-encompassing love I had before. This new love is quieter, more reserved, but still good love. I have learned to thrive with a broken heart.

A broken heart is still broken, yet broken hearts can be loved and be in love again!

THE BATHROBE

Doreen Day

Chastised for not being extroverted, it's deeply haunting that I failed telling you how much I love you. Many occasions I couldn't. I held my feelings in reserve. Somewhere in a space where no one could judge. No one could take what I feel and destroy it. Condemn or disrespect it.

I was terrified to express my feelings, fearing blowback.

I wasn't encouraged to love people openly. You know that. You couldn't fully nurture me, either. Not completely. We lived in a place where abuse and dysfunction rooted, smothered and often times, killed that which otherwise would be beautiful, normal and right.

Before your death, you said you knew I loved you, but I had an odd way of showing it. True. In my world, actions of love are far stronger than words.

With your passing, I feel such a deep sense of loss. I ask myself, "would I feel more peace if I had been brought up under different circumstances? Void of abuse that has tried and, at times, been successful suppressing my true self."

I find comfort wrapping myself in your bathrobe in the wee hours of the morning. Standing in the darkness gazing at the stars. Admiring the freedom of the universe. Wondering if you can hear me. Or see me muddling to find my way during this harsh time. I hope you are gently holding my hand in my sleep, asking that I release the guilt I feel for failing to tell you I love you.

Remember when we laughed about funny things, rode through the fields with the sun on our backs, cried together at the loss of a four-legged friend?

Remember how we huddled together after a violent family explosion? How we talked at the breakfast table alone for hours over cinnamon toast? I don't remember either of us saying, "I love you" much. I'm so very sorry, Mom.

I'll continue to wrap myself tightly in your robe and gaze at the stars. Whispering "I love you."

Hear me, please.

TEXAS TOAST AND NARCISSISTIC YOU

Doreen Day

I tried. I tried again. And again.
Blind to your narcissism. Trapped by your gaslighting.
YOU cried victim! Kicked my soul. Bruised my being.
Belittled my inspiration, my light, my sensuality.
                            Fed it to the fire ants.
                            Destroyed my trust.
While you swirled your charm upon others.
Manipulated my thoughts till confusion pushed me to the brink.
                            Afraid, low, defeated... my heart still beat.
                            Escaped. My quiet plan.
Left you standing empty. Probably not for long.
I scraped your dirt off my boots. Burned your Texas toast.
I didn't get the lies. I didn't get the deceit. I do now.
I forgave myself, my stupidity, my naiveté.
Learned to love myself again.
Even after being stung by an old evil scorpion like you.

PENCILS IN MY NOSE

Doreen Day

I know her heart ramps up when we talk. Her eyes illuminate when something funny comes from me. We orbit each other. Dance like two butterflies in summer. Time cupped both of us and took us to this point. A position of truth and confession.

I love her, the closest of friend. Even sister. I know she is there for me. Supports, believes and encourages gently, quietly. Honestly.

She loves me not only as a friend, but with hopes of me becoming her sustained lover. Her companion. Her shoulder, her hero. I understand with whole heart.

If we were lovers, perhaps we would be two goddesses shining, glistening as waves crash beneath our feet. Sand tickling as it escapes from between our toes, flows back to the ocean floor. We would be intoxicated on each other and the scent of the salt water trickling along our bodies.

Maybe, we would be content spooning while reading to each other on a lazy Sunday morning, sipping sweet coffee. Watching mid-night movies during the winter cold while frost kisses flowers left from late summer and the stars ache sharply for our attention.

Maybe there would be the most tender understanding when one or both our lives are shaken by an outside intruder or threatened by unforeseen complications. Comforting freely. Protecting each other with healing qualities, aiming to find the light. The way.

Together, giggling uncontrollably over something so funny that we almost pee our pants. I suppose that could happen. We are over sixty...We might be goofy, extraordinarily silly and exceedingly funny. Like putting pencils up my nose to catch her attention.

The most painful, difficult thing for me is to know she wishes our lives, our ideals, our preferences were different, yet the same. That we share the same sexuality. Woman to woman.

We can't change who we are. Can't always become something we are not. But we can accept and love even if it is not wholly what we hoped for.

If I were to change my sexuality to prefer women, that woman would be you.

SUSTAINS

Doreen Day

Amber light accentuates masculine features. Life chatters outside these walls. Do passers-by hear us during morning stroll? Wrens downstairs gossip while primping lavender hair. Curls blow under silver bullets. Oh! If they only knew what passion warms above! Your voice easy, affirms.

Love wanders freely.
Anxious hands have no boundaries.
Glide along sultry skin.

Resting in crisp cotton, talk about now, then, someday. Maybe sooner. We tease, tweak and coo. Play until something ignites as life sustains and the sun fills our small smoldering room. Light hides nothing in shadow. Humidity trickles, shines smooth skin and muscle.

Love wanders freely.
Breath and kisses turbulent.
Limbs supple catch fire.

Bodies' sleek union, quenching souls' thirst, while eyes confess long awaited. Love rolls tight as sidewalk laughter rides soft breeze. Sweet exhaustion spoons. Sun finds shade in sleep.

Love wanders freely.

DOVE'S VOICE

Doreen Day

I lay in tall grass listening to a Mourning Dove in tall pines. Warm breezes caress my face as supple blades of grass sway.

The memory of your touch, sound of your voice, your essence, linger in a corner of my being, like a best friend. Your image makes love to my heart. Stirs my gut. Nourishes my soul.

The dove sings slow, deep with haunting truth about love and loss.

I am euphoria. I am pain.
I am the driving force of passion.
I am what takes your breath away.
I am the foundation to heal, sacrifice and serve.
I am the endless blanket of compassion, empathy and understanding.

I AM LOVE.

OLD SOUL

Doreen Day

Eyes dance fire. Ignite.
Energy propels soul's flight.
Red socks tap love's light.

PRIMAL

Doreen Day

Aurora Borealis in the fall sky,
Spooning beneath a blanket.
Steamed breath escapes in darkness.

Cold ground warms while
Waves of vibrant greens, blues and violets
Swirl wildly under night's canopy.

Screech owls loquacious
Distant coyotes primitive voices
Sweet nuzzles propose play.

Passionate. Unrestrained.
Waves green, blue and violet swirl
Wild like Aurora Borealis in fall sky.

LOVE NEVER RUSTS

Doreen Day

Remember when we met? I asked you to dance. You were stunned.

Remember how you helped me through the darkest days of college?

Remember when we found passion in unexpected places?

Remember I told you how sexy your legs were when you dressed for work?

Remember how we talked for hours while I bathed after days of straight study?

Remember how we decided to live together? We were jubilant!

Remember the moment you asked me to marry you? We cried.

Remember how you said you understood me? You did.

Remember how we believed in each other?

Remember what it felt like to be apart from each other?

Remember how strained our relationship became as time went on? It was.

Remember how troubled you grew and alcohol became your lover?

Remember how we talked about me leaving? I did.

Remember how we wanted to make it work?

Remember, over the decades, we still loved each other unconditionally?

Remember when you married and had a son? I was happy you found life.

Remember when you called me August 31, 1994? Seemingly together.

Remember when you pulled the trigger that night? I can hear, see and smell it.

I still remember how I couldn't get my breath when I received my letter addressed to you, "Deceased. Returned to sender" in my mailbox.

I know the pain, sorrow, guilt… I know the continual love of a man who took his life because he couldn't find the light. The hope.

Twenty-seven years later, I remember you…

COSMIC COMICS

Jeffrey Ferebee

I sent my son some comic books, a letter, and some poetry after leaving one Saturday in June bleeding, with his mother screaming help as she ran out the door behind me, running with a duffel's worth of clothes towards my car.

That evening I checked into the county jail and spent the next 48 hours on the floor considering the previous 24.

Now, the comic books were a bit much considering I'd sent him Guardians of the Galaxy, Ms. Marvel, the Hulk, and Batman. See, in the psyche of a comic book, something of an enigma occurs. A phenomenon for the sake of story, a journey between viewer and medium - same as a painting acting as a portal.

In fact, the one you're entering now paints the same story, different medium. Suffering so gold shines on everything and everyone.

Being a book and music store attendant places one amongst the greatest creators of all time. Mozart, Alexander Dumas, Raymond Carver, Miles Davis…. The greatest surrealists, impressionists, waiting in their created forms upon the shelf. By the door waits a security man with a taser and master level ability to make small talk.

At the register waits yours truly, the final gatekeeper for your media if you don't count the taser. Standing watch, sending disciples to their homes with Charlie Parker and Monet, medicine prescribed by the individual artist.

One day, beyond the register's beeps and bells bouncing lovely people through the capital gains of art's gate stood a giant man handing a note to me, saying in perfect penmanship: "if you love your family, give me the cash in your register and I'll be on my way.

I have a gun."

He stood there looking at me looking at him holding the note and I thought about my son and the letter his mother wrote to me regarding the creations I sent my son. Gun to my head: "send child support to your son's college fund or send books about adjusting to change, big emotions, self-control, coping skills and how families look different versus toys and fun stuff…that he cannot act out by yelling or putting his hands on others has been hard for him to understand." Send the money and we'll be on our way.

So the process was easy for me.

The burly man did not discharge his weapon and add years to a prison sentence, he got the money from my drawer in less than 15 seconds and tucked the money into this magnificent strapped bag on his belly, closed his coat and was down the street getting into his Tahoe by one minute, 20 seconds.

He glided like Hermes and forever now, since that cold night in February, a great big, burly god fetches my hourly earnings from the bookstore and drives like hell through the night listening to Kendrick Lamar and smoking cigarettes to deliver child support to my son's home in the Carolinas.

He only stops to use the restroom and he's always on time. Better than any operating system, so my kid can travel the world and figure out the future in 2035. Then, my son will visit me at the bookstore, at my register, and we can cry together about the moments we lost in the great war of time and love.

I'll invite him to dinner at my apartment and he'll say he's got a flight to catch.

FOUND

Jeffrey Ferebee

These lines to report, you came
to the right place, time.
To say who you are is more than okay.
Far more, far out.
Stay a moment and breathe.

Heavy hearts need gravity's tug.
No place to be but being.
This space is the universe
leaving you a love note.
Are you listening?

Stuff of stars in your bloodstream, friend…
Not beating darkness, but
being light and love
as a result of its magnitude.

Wrapping warm words 'round cool
bodies bruised busy by bursts of energy,
run ragged, thought tragic.
Billed breathing small print
history of who you
really are.

COSMIC CONSCIOUSNESS

Jeffrey Ferebee

Driving to nature's stairs, golden hour of sunshine.
Dog sensed darkness and flipped the route to going back.

Marveled stone and man made
structure but, you, looking behind crimson
hair to say, "All eternity, dear?"

Phenomena love playing hide and seek
amnesia: thou art that.

No assembly required.
Anything else is noise.
Blind narcissus walking
backwards over a cliff.
Love yourself first and others will follow.

Here love sings,
hymns light
orange gates
peach pink.
Blink, it's
here.

LOVE GHOST

Jeffrey Ferebee

Love is the decision to keep going
regardless of dying. It is few words
said over your grave.
It is crying.

Hugging your neck like a grandmother
bringing far off messages of "let go."

Love's a razor staying sharp on passion. It's deputies
coming to break up the racket. Love's raw and real...
It too can die.

Harder than hate, it requires feelings, courage, guts...
It's not corporate, not analysis, not software.
It's taking time off to figure out what to think and
do next. Leaning into the blindness of
truth's bruise.
It's talking this shit out, asking for help. It's admitting
you were wrong – challenging yourself.

ALBATROSS

Jeffrey Ferebee

Little love, can you make it pause?
This one stops, that one goes.
This thinks, that knows.
Wonder what echoes
souls to hate what's different?
Identified by dying flesh at life's pasture;
Forgetting they too were once a child,
loving time and space
wild, no boundaries, nobody
to say who you ought to be.
Not this one, that one,
Albatross. Spinning rings around
Saturn in your sleep;
Steeping mountains
leading sheep.

MY FIRST REAL KISS

Alice Flowers

He was a tall glass of chocolate—chocolate milk, cool and smooth. To give you a visual, he was the black version of John Travolta in the movie, *Saturday Night Fever. He walked like and was as smooth as John Travolta's move character Tony Manero.*

His name is Jim C. and he stole my heart. I was in the 10th grade and was drawn to his "bad boy" persona. He was so very cool, laid back, respectful, and pleasant to be around. Even though JC had a bad-boy image, he ignored the attention and never took advantage of his status with the girls. He could have had almost any girl in school, but he wasn't interested in having a lot of girlfriends just because he could. He was sure of himself and not fazed by all of the attention...that was attractive to me.

I got his attention and we flirted in the hallways and during Woodshop. His smile could melt ice sheets in East Antarctica and he knew it. You can imagine how it felt when he would grab my hands and smile my way. His cool demeanor could not go unnoticed. He was so cool that he didn't even attend his own high school graduation. He didn't think it was necessary so they mailed his diploma to him.

After he graduated, our connection went from immature flirting in the hallways at school to late-night phone calls. I'm sure most people believe that a 16/17-year-old can't possibly fall in love. We may not understand love at that age, but we certainly can feel the effects of its emotions.

I will always remember our first kiss. It happened at 175 Charles Ave. in St. Paul, Minnesota. We were hanging out on the front porch at my Mother's house. That is where he kissed me for the first time. It was like fireworks on the fourth of July...going off around us! He never tried anything past us kissing, holding hands, laughing, and talking together, because he knew I wasn't that kind of girl. He asked if he could wear my graduation ring. There was a time when a boy wore your graduation ring, you knew you were the One.

I will always remember Jim C. and our first kiss.

HE NEVER LOVED ME!

Alice Flowers

"Let everyone know that this one is mine."

That's what he said to a group of guy friends as I walked toward them on my way to an audition. That's what one of his friends who was with him that day shared with me.

I was 21. He was 41. I was naïve. He was a Casanova.

I didn't know who he was and I certainly had never considered dating a man 20 years my senior. I had no idea how deliberate his intentions were. He flirted with me with his eyes, his flirtatious smile, his cool demeanor... Yes, I was enamored by his charisma.

The next time I saw him was at an afternoon baseball game. He invited me to meet him at a local bar. I shouldn't have gone, but I couldn't say 'No' to him. He was handsome, smart and paid attention to me. His debonair tactics had worked. His words charmed me.

He said, "Well, we meet again. I haven't been able to get you off my mind since the first time I saw you."

Even though I had a baby at age 18, I had lived a sheltered life. So, I fell for his lies and wanted to see him every waking moment.

By the time I realized he had multiple girlfriends, I was in too deep. He convinced, persuaded, induced, bamboozled me to look the other way. Even though I would have never accepted this behavior from a boy my age, I painfully did from him. I was young and naïve; he was older and experienced; he knew how to control my mind.

How did I get away?

My older sister saw how emotionally destroyed I had become. She knew this guy and knew that I was no match for him. So, she had a conversation and asked him to stay away from me, that I was too young for him. He told her he had me wrapped around his finger and that I was not going anywhere. And told her there was nothing she could do about it.

"Watch me take her away from you," my sister told him.

With his usual smirk, he replied, "Try it."

By this time, I was tired of hurting and was ready to get away, but didn't have the courage to do so. With my sister's help, I found the strength to get away from the selfish man who never loved me.

Many years later, the lessons are clear.

"Sweet words are not love."

"Watch who you think you love."

SELF-BETRAYAL...

...my journey from self-doubt to self-assurance

Alice Flowers

I needed validation from other people because I didn't trust my own decisions. I would never make decisions without getting approval from others. I constantly second guessed myself with a lot of negative "what ifs..." From a young age, I wanted to own my own business one day. But the "what ifs" got in the way.

What if they think I'm not qualified, blah, blah, blah. The big one, though, was what if they think I am a fraud? That stopped me cold in my tracks from pursuing my dream of owning my own business. I looked confident on the outside but was insecure on the inside. That fear caused me to put my dream on hold for many years. I betrayed my dream and sabotaged my belief with negative self-talk. "Alice, you don't deserve to own your own business." "You have nothing to offer." All the while, I longed to be the CEO of my own company.

What an oxymoron! Wanting to own my own business, but too afraid to pursue it... Talk about self-betrayal at its fullest level.

I confirmed my negative thoughts by my lifestyle choices. I surrounded myself with people who did not dream or were too afraid to pursue their dreams. We found it easier to just live in the moment. I kept my dream alive through sheer determination and willpower that one day I will have the courage to go for it.

I kept my dream alive for 40 years. I worked on my confidence, even when it was painful to do so. I changed my surroundings, started investing in myself, read books, and invested in coaching programs. I discovered what was holding me back.

I was shy.

I discovered that I was working from a place of timidity, hence the reason I felt the need to be validated. I no longer feel the need to be validated before I take action. No more self-betrayal. I not only look the part, but I now feel the part, and am the part.

My determination kept my dream alive, but it was my willpower that took me forward to now owning my own business. I was determined to find a way out of self-betrayal and the willpower to love me enough to find the strength to win.

I Love Alice! I am Alice! I am a Winner!

IF LOVE IS... a poem to my future

Alice Flowers

If love is arms I want around me right now, then they would belong to you, my future

If love is being together, then you are the One.

If your love whispers in my ear, I hear the strength of the ocean, the softness of the sea

If love is the color Red, it would be exciting and powerful to give in to you

If love is kind, if love is gentle, if love is forgiving, I want it to be a soft cool breeze in summer, under an old oak tree, in a hammock swing, napping with you

Love is you, galloping toward me ever so gallantly, whisking me into your arms without restraint... you are my knight, chivalry is back, I love it...

And honoring the old love song, I proclaim: If love is wrong, I don't want to be right. Not now, not ever...

If love is meant for me to show my vulnerabilities... you better love me back because I'm a hot mess!

If love is strong, then why do I feel helpless in your arms, my future?

If love is to love others as you would want them to love you, then I'm all in

If you think love is overrated and you need to believe, listen to the Gregory Porter song, *If Love is Overrated*...

If you want me and you believe love is a song, I will compose the lyrics to your love song?

THERE AND NOT THERE

John Masson

Daydreams and stubborn thinking fraught with never reality,
Thoughts of us connected, lasting conversations
Blending our minds, brisk morning walks in chilled light;
Gazing together across waterscapes viewing urban twilights
Before anxious lips brace and meet; wanting rainbows sing anew.
Only love and hurt remain when life goes and heaven takes us in.

Close, but far, never near enough to create possibility;
To embrace, rummage your locks, massage soft skin
That bubbles, echoing with hope of sanctioned long days
Of searching and holding; when joy tears align as stars;
When burdens, reality and inhibitions flee from sight;
Feelings open and erupt - a raging fire burns and cares.

I know your voice, have heard its tenderness, its
Joy and remorse, its tension, sadness and purity;
When your heart cares, how it loves laughter;
When it looks away, choosing not to cause hurt
Without assumption or heaped praise. Whether love, loneliness
Or desire, must I gaze away amid dreams of never?

QUICK at 3

John Masson

Thinking about sex mornings, afternoons and nights?
Why not? That's what creates offspring, saucy moans
And euphoria. Better than lazy afternoon naps and tea
Or mad weeks, months or years of anticipation dreams...
Cuddling, rubbing, cooing, holding...
This is pure intimacy, what life is, what love should be...
Affection's flashing lights, its finest hour;
It's truth or myth that entanglement brings quick sleep.
Yet afraid to talk about sex in our colonials and purist towns
Though podcasts, magazines and online posts chatter like crows
While those in other worlds prance naked, showing
Shameless bodies and counseling teens with open talks.
Decades ago hippies had free love that vanished, I guess, with age...
Did anyone proclaim that "use it or lose it?" applies to sex?
Is this a rash poem speaking truth for those believing that
Sex is young, regular, agile, impulsive and forever lost after
Sag and gray emerge and worst friends push lingering age jokes?
Or, negative inner-self barks, telling us we're old and done!
Oh! So, sorry people! I forgot sex is whispered only in bedrooms.
Wake up humanity, burn your prudish, false morality and
Risk-averse selves. Get sex - get hot, get naked - or stay dressed?
C'mon! Got 15 minutes for afternoon tea, a nap and a quickie?

MID-BOOK BREAK

Never heard of a Mid-Book Break before, neither have we. Laughter...

What's wrong with a **few** questions or providing Good Partner tips to keep your mind racing and further amp up your emotions in the middle of a book about relationships? And, to get couples in the mood for date night or a special occasion after-party dessert, we've added our favorite love songs.

1. Is your spouse or partner your best friend?
2. Mention one positive and one negative way the 2020-2021 pandemic have affected relationships with your spouse, partner or family?
3. Does your face most often reveal the stress or pleasure of your relationship?
4. Can couples love each another and not be "in love" with each another?
5. Are you lonely and in love or lonely seeking love?
6. Do you keep secrets from your spouse or partner?
7. Is it time for you to make a major confession to yourself and your partner?
8. Why is social media the worst medium for weak relationships?
9. Is it ideal for best friends to date or fall in love?
10. What has this book told you about your relationships?
11. Have you given up on finding the right one?
12. Name the three (3) best things about your current relationship?
13. Do you want to live longer than your partner or spouse?
14. Can you discuss politics, race and gender issues with your partner or spouse?
15. Could you have a serious relationship with someone 15 years older or 10 years younger than you?

TRUE? FALSE?

1. Fifty percent of all relationships involve more chaos than calm.
2. A broken heart is the worst kind of grief.
3. Race, gender, age or orientation should never hinder real love.
4. Who you live with is often not who you love.
5. Kissing is the most important part of intimacy.
6. A relationship with four ears is one that lasts.
7. It's better to be alone and happy than together and unhappy.
8. Prayer, meditation and truth keep relationships intact.
9. Fifty is the most mentally daunting age for women.
10. A woman knows when her man is lying.
11. Lying and blame are easier than truth and admission.
12. Health is 100 times better than wealth.
13. Most men know little about women's bodies.
14. A good marriage can last forever.
15. Receiving a love letter or poem is forever precious.
16. Your friends and family are destroying your relationship.
17. Talking is better than walking away.
18. A good relationship helps physical health and longevity.
19. When the fire goes, the relationship goes.
20. Somewhere in the world there's a special one for everyone.

GOOD PARTNER TRAITS

1. Knows no man or woman or relationship is perfect.
2. A good partner laughs more than they growl, complain or blame.
3. A good partner never judges or berates you.
4. A good partner enjoys what you enjoy and has their own likes.
5. A good partner is beautiful or handsome in their own way.
6. A good partner is mature.
7. An older partner is okay if they are mentally, physically, emotionally fit. Don't be afraid of an age gap. Be afraid of a maturity gap.
8. A good partner knows a great relationship can come in any color, race, age or orientation.
9. A good partner lets you vent when necessary.
10. A good partner grows to admire and love your children.
11. Both partners strive to stay emotionally, mentally and physically healthy.
12. Communicates openly and challenges the other to do the same.
13. Respects your history, your work and your moods...
14. Will not overwhelm your personality. A partner who controls their emotions.
15. A pragmatic thinker who is not afraid to defend when necessary.
16. Someone who has their partner's security in mind.
17. Smart, but doesn't wear it on their sleeve. Not a "know-it-all."
18. A good partner is your Number One supporter.
19. You come FIRST!
20. Apologizes in a timely manner without being asked.
21. Kindness. No naysayers or blamers.

22. Humor. Is able to laugh at themselves first.

23. Intelligent, with real life street smarts; can play in jeans or a suit...

24. A good partner is always happy to see you.

25. Someone who admires your intellect every day.

26. Cherishes each day with you like it's their last.

27. Enjoys your body. Excited to give and receive your pleasure.

28. Is mentally tough. Doesn't wilt under pressure. No whiners.

29. Doesn't emotionally disappear, ghost or play immature games.

30. Wants you to outlive them.

31. Will tell you in person if the relationship is not working.

32. Is not a shiny penny with fast talk, flash and no substance.

33. Enjoys deep conversations, easy TV nights and cooking together.

34. Is unafraid to reveal personal struggles.

35. Has overcome struggles through hard work, self-belief and grit.

36. Believes in you more than themselves.

37. Knows you are a "catch."

FAVORITE (sad and wonderful) LOVE SONGS

I Will Always Love You – Whitney Houston
Silly Love Songs – Paul McCartney
How Deep Is Your Love – The Bee Gees
Anticipation – Carly Simon
Misty – Johnny Mathis
Fly Me To The Moon – Frank Sinatra
Unchained Melody – The Righteous Brothers
Unforgettable – Nat King Cole
The Thrill Is Gone – B.B. King
Mr. Sandman – The Chordettes
All In Love Is Fair – Nancy Wilson
September Song – Walter Huston
Sideways – Santana
A House Is Not a Home – Luther Vandross
You Are So Beautiful – Joe Cocker
The Old Rugged Cross – George Bennanard
Always – Bon Jovi
The Way We Were – Barbara Steisand
The Shadow of Your Smile – Astrud Gilberto and Stan Getz
Iris – Goo Goo Dolls
Stay In My Corner – The Dells
The Closer I Get to You – Roberta Flack and Donny Hathaway
Change The World – Eric Clapton
Anything For You – Gloria Estefan
So I Could Find My Way – Enya
All Woman – Lisa Stansfield
Something Just Like This – Coldplay and The Chainsmokers
I Don't Want to Miss A Thing – Aerosmith
Poetry Man – Phoebe Snow
My Cherie Amour – Stevie Wonder
You've Lost That Lovin' Feelin – The Righteous Brothers
Where Is The Love? – Roberta Flack and Donny Hathaway
The One I Love – David Gray
Fire & Desire – Teena Marie and Rick James
Live Like You Were Dying – Tim McGraw
All of Me – John Legend
I Only Have Eyes For You – The Flamingos
Why Do Fools Fall In Love? – Frankie Lymon & The Teenagers
I Can't Make You Love Me – Will Downing

OMNIPRESENT

Lori Myers

Summer breezes
In the mid of the night
Lightning in the distance
The sky shifts about
Leaves rustling overhead
Light whispering sounds
Tiny raindrops fall upon my face
Warmth envelops me
Gazing at the stars
I see your loving face
Closing my eyes
I hear your soothing tones
Embracing my place in the world
I am not alone
Your Presence Surrounds Me!

OH, HOW I LOVE A DAY AT THE BEACH!

Lori Myers

crashing waves
giggling teenage girls
rumbling thunder in the distance
aromatic suntan lotion
freshly caught fish
salty crustaceans litter the beach
flying kites and fishing poles
bocce ball, boogie boards, buckets of seashells
bicycles, runners, excited toddlers chasing seagulls
carefree, frolicking, merriment...
no cares, no fear, no masks
COVID free for a bit...

DEAR DAD

Lori Myers

Not a day goes by that you're not with me.

Deep, emotional revelations still come - large, small, with

tears, most filled with laughter, sometimes with regret.

Virtues I hold dear you imparted on me. Not so many words,

but actions. What I thought was inherently me is a mirror of you.

Strength doesn't need to be loud, overbearing, in your face;
it can be quiet, steady, and resilient.
Kindness doesn't need recognition or motivation;
it shows love in the simplest, subtle, yet impactful ways.
Duty isn't old fashioned or out of style;
it grounds us to purpose higher than our own –
faith, family, and community.
Humor doesn't need to be vulgar, cruel, or at someone's expense;
a good practical joke gives everyone a hearty laugh.
Love doesn't always show up as flowers and chocolates;
it may not come with words,
but to listen, to guide, to counsel, to uplift.

Here and the hereafter are separated only by a curtain,

so, I hope you hear me from your heavenly place. I'm certain I never

really thanked you or gave you the credit you deserved. Yet, I am thankful,

and blessed beyond measure for the love you gave in so many ways.

Forever know that your LOVE is your legacy!

REVELATION

Lori Myers

At times, I've been lost and confused
Searching to fill the hollowness
Real happiness just out of reach;
Relying on material things to close the void.

When I found the love of the Lord
Emptiness and uncertainty vanished
Once my heart was opened
What love IS and IS NOT became clear.

I learned to give, not gain
To smile, not cry
To pray, not carry my burdens alone
To humble myself before God.

Sincere love was being conceived
Without my works involved
Complete now, I cherish the blessing
My love for you eternal!

RESURGENCE

Lori Myers

Winter approaches, life is muted
Succumbing, surrendering, sleeping...
Incubation, silence, reflection...
A new day, a new hope.

Kindness, dignity, grace
Revived, renewed, refreshed
Winter no more.

UNFOLDING

Marisa Porto

How do you know
what will happen
when the sun rises
or the night falls?

There are no certainties
in the world
except the tide, death
and you.

Your voice
soft and warm
moves me to open
an unclenched fist;
a sharp and sudden unfolding.

I wonder,
is this how a flower feels
emerging
into the light?

WITHOUT

Marisa Porto

I woke this morning to
bills, appointments, dogs waiting to be fed.
I lose myself in paperwork
until there is nothing left to do
but pack the box with the antique wine glass
your mother gave to me before she died.
It sat for years in my kitchen
reminding me of her, of you
"I want it kept in the family," she said.

Last night
I explained to a friend
I feel without.
There is no better word.
Without the light through the window
or the African sunflowers bending
over the back fence,
without dancing in the parking lot,
or combining lips and hips,
without a baby
born red and ripe
and bloodied with the death of possibility.

These days, I explain,
Without is a verb.
It reaches through the past
and into the chest.
It tears out this trembling heart.

BEYOND THE WORDS

Marisa Porto

Each days begins
the same
waking
to this ache
for you.
You smell
of baby powder and sex.
My morning coffee...
But this day requires
concentration
on the sentence
the paragraph
the story. I push you
a-w-a-y
with work
and words
and work some more
until I fall
into the daydream
of your arms.

Today
I cannot find the strength
to give more to my love
for words.
I do not want
the strength
to give less
To the thought
of you.

ILLUSION

Marisa Porto

Ten years later,
In the middle of the night,
I am on the phone with a friend.
This is when you text to say,
"I am not pining for you.
There is nothing to resolve."
Today is your birthday.
You are sitting on the porch
drinking
and thinking of us.
Meanwhile, Mary
is on the phone crying,
her husband is lying
in a hospital bed,
his kidneys failing,
his heart dying,
the light lessening
in his bright eyes.
She kissed him goodnight,
He grabbed her hand.
"I don't want to leave you," he said.

THE RED ROOM

Marisa Porto

The importance of that
red room
Was not in what was said
Or done
breath on breast, hand to hip
moving toward
and then away.
It lay in the epilogue,
when you turned,
and the back of you was
all I could hear.

BLACK BOXES

Marisa Porto

Studies of black boxes
show pilots call out for
their mothers before they die.
I think of this as my mother
thrashes late into the night
at a hospital
where no one knows
how to pronounce her name.
She is calling out,
for a dead aunt, a brother, her mother who
died of the same disease.
She loses her English in the morphine
as she loses herself.
I hold her hand and wonder...
Will I do this too when I am dying?
Will I cry out for a woman
with whom I shared nothing
but a lost language
and a predisposition
for a long and
painful death.

MASTECTOMY

Marisa Porto

She feels the nub
That was once her breast and
asks,
"What do you think?"
moving her hand
against the raw, stapled line
left and under her armpit.
I look at the site of what was once
a 38D. My 32Bs still intact.
I pause to consider how
to respond as I pull her shirt back
into place.
"I think after all these years,
we finally look alike," I say.
It makes me smile
when she laughs.

BEHIND THE MASK (a short trilogy)

Glenn Proctor

Behind centuries of invisible masks humanity rests, blinders and actions strategic, peace and love buckling, covered and uncovered faces denigrating disciples, derelicts and decency in one swath. Comfort and survival rest behind eyes, undeterred by lies...

You behind the mask, me behind the mask, men behind the mask, women behind the mask... lovers hiding secrets and woe behind the mask... Love is a mask? What's hidden behind your mask?

Masks are social virus, men and women, positioned arbiters of morality and empathy; love hollow as fallen trees in hearts and minds where hypocrisy whips, running faster than speeding tsunamis.
As frenetic societies cripple; bodies crumble like sand castles.

Today's normal is a masquerade ball; a daily dance of Halloween in plain sight, regret and love in the same song, poems without endings, sentences blurred in mid-stream, fantasy hugs and prayers for whose purpose? Verbal masks hide truths; lay angrily awake in quiet beds.

Humanity thrives as mask, as old as pharaoh, alive as tomorrow's next breath... without apology, our masks thrive, hiding love and truth... Invisible, or not, but lasting...

BEHIND THE MASK II

while walking my dog at 7:27 a.m. on March 6, 2021 at a strip mall near my house, I saw more than a dozen masks littering the ground...

Glenn Proctor

What color is your mask today?
What fear and secrets hide beneath?
Yet discarding neither fantasy nor fancy,
      the mask forever lives, past virus and distance;
      invisible and present; bold, raw, often implicit...
      sanctioning the few as equal and hope fade...

Do you not love earth?
      wishing to make it social debris,
      like the many who suffer with
      rigid eyes still upon them?

BEHIND THE MASK III

Glenn Proctor

Behind the mask we all stand,
        in silence, in loud portrayal, life's
        actors spilling cautious words,
        rousing threats; uncertainty's veil
        covered, neither naked or shamed…

Who is your neighbor, your lover, your friend
        to be so blunt in costume and mask of today?
        Is house not a home, this nation not sanctuary
        where love and right have some meaning?

Which man, which woman cries behind the mask, speaking softly…
        unhinging nerves with eruption language,
        thinking lover is gone, praying or lost the thrill;
        seeing families and friends disrupted by creeping drama.

Who hides behind position, yet hopes not to be recognized,
        burning decades of laws and societal bridges like eternal
        flames…
        love masks, a thousand fields of charred paper and cloth…

Behind the mask we all stand and hide…
        And live without apology…

QUESTION?

(Written in 1988 and published in 2014 in **KICKING BOTTLES, NEWS & DUST – An Autobiography**, the first of the **FINDING DUST TRILOGY**)

Glenn Proctor

Love makes us grin;
Love makes us cry;
Love makes us thin;
Love makes us fly;
Love makes us sin;
Love makes us die;
Love makes us win;
Love makes us sigh;
Love makes us think.
Why do we love?

LEFT HISTORY

Glenn Proctor

All the 20ish and 30ish *girls*
with five and six letter names
came quickly to anxious summers...
the front door absorbing bold knocks;
hair brown and flowing,
tinted blondes with short cuts;
an assortment of soft skin colors
giving lush hugs seeking return;
flashing flirts with full eyes
dancing to midnight silence
keeping distance to avoid another touch;
leaving quickly without words.

The woman came slowly
from icy air to
join later years of pretend
to applaud levity
to fix mental warts
to adorn and satisfy
before leaving quickly
without closing the side door.

LOVE FALLING, LOVE RISING

Glenn Proctor

Love rises, has big risks, appears unexplained when friendship
Begins and infatuation grows like young roses.
Is humanity ever ready for love? Real love, lasting love..?

Love smiles and falls, makes its own truth, hovers years over curious
Hearts with questions often unanswered. Who really knows the other?

Love is recess rising, silly laughter aplenty; maturity with kid play
Finding swings, late TV and chocolate cookies, warm and fresh.
Memories are bitter and sweet, lasting for eons.

Love is clear eyes supporting reality; emotions jumping like beans
Minds, at times, unattended – not one way or the other...
Who is ever ready for strong talk and difficult lasting decisions?

Love has stops, one-way signs within desired expectations not met
In the middle, two finding reality comes with surprising risks;
With curved lines that scrap and blunt life's straight and narrow.
Find soft words said for right; a cherished something to believe in.

When love is two-way, body and mind juices flow into soft spaces
From pleasured moves. Light moans spark unbroken ecstasy.
Love is hot, tongues raging volcanoes spilling on breasts and thighs
Making bright faces. Love lips lock; searching for heated zones.

Cherish self and those who love you; go wild when curtains fall;
And drop like autumn crimson, revealing health and yearning.
All ages can rise and flourish; together walks are rhythm with daring.

Let loving hearts run as utopian days, like paced marathons;
Love is success with suns; friendly rain, fresh like quick showers;
The days when lives breathe and glow; burning with fierce
Intensity, desire and hope. A time to smile and forever ask:
What is love? Why do we love?

MORE?

Glenn Proctor

Too late, your blood and bone now dust, remnants of humanity that toiled,
    spoiled, splashed and spilled reality like sunny day ice drips;
    wishes for peace stumbled, verbal taunts exploded as war, the Golden Rule too often smashed like young marauders with fresh pumpkins.

With closed eyes, wishes now blow like tumbleweeds passing, once
    obvious feelings and thoughts staggering past Judgment Day,
    the reckoning closing doors, unannounced... generational
    narcissists and their kind wallowing in hell's abyss

Too late to love; or care enough to undo one's attitude of wrath
    your mind boards wiped clean, power and reliance rock
    still, bones and blood a dark ebony; old news of abrupt endings
    without repeats, do-overs and second chance fantasies...

Perhaps, the gone wish for one last feeling, death's final makeup call;
    the Spirit's final yearning, the short apology for not loving;
    a soft message for those busy, brash and disconnected...
    'tis Heaven's concluding favor, a forever peace ...
    the gone wishing they had time to love more.

NEVER TOGETHER, ALWAYS TOGETHER

Mother Gertrude - Dec 1947 / Father Clyde - Feb 1991 / Sister Claudia – Mar 2013

Glenn Proctor

Years of curiosity and uncertainty / connections casual like seeing

Friends on weekends / adult phone calls tinged with curiosity, some

laughter, basic talk about kids, missing history and Aunt Elsie...

So much why remains / mysterious like the names in this poem...

Didn't know you well enough as parents and only sibling / good intentions

Blurred / absent years / each of us living our version of adulthood.

Did I really grieve and say goodbye? Was there love or friendship?

Names and blood shared / four adult bodies lined with kidney and

Heart disease, diabetes... a malady never spoken...

Why take mother away before my 18-month eyes could admire

her love and beauty? The time before I went from family to foster care.

Tipped quite a few with Clyde / played occasional pool / talked sports

Never much talk about life / Mom / Elaine or what he cared about.

Never saw me win medals or chide me about regular Cs and Ds.

Like fathers and sons back then, he didn't say / I didn't ask.

Got closer to Claudia as we aged / still not enough time or talk to

Know her soul / yet her aspirations for the girls concise and clear...

Three smart women, her legacy sealed in love

Claudia rests with pride... smiles of appreciation...

As she and the parents look down... waiting

For the four of us to become whole; sharing love for the first time.

SEARCH & SURVIVAL & SANITY

Glenn Proctor

'Tis said to be the dangerous – greatest of emotions and sin;
Far past our flirting, infatuations, hard kisses, maybes and flings;
Affection that absorbs, turning old and young bodies into masses of fire.
The focused search for love is often unspoken amid silent pursuit;
Yet some prefer risqué running and riches than as couple at rest.

As we search, we survive, resilience abuzz in busy and daily pursuits
Wishing for hope, enough of chemistry's sign – beyond friendly heartbeats
For sanity's sake; embraced pulses racing with belief. Is the when now?
Yet waiting is ever exhausting and evil; misery horrid and haunting when
Thrust-awake dreams map situations not yet realized or imagined.

Love is a thief, the bridge that bends darkness, above calamity to calm;
That knocks and doesn't knock - that frees, sleeps and holds others hostage;
That satisfies like bitter chocolate; relief for bones sagging without pleasure.
Half love lingers, wavers like untuned pianos; lonely ones burdened with rings or
No rings. So much unsaid when surviving, searching and climbing past fences;
Bottomless oceans bring the right catch; or for some, the best get away.

Searching for love, as with humans, all beasts and things of this earth;
A devotion calming anxiety; support when fear and faint voices are tears;
Does love have an age, a time or a line, picking the right one off sanity's shelf?
The single ones wanting; couples wandering curious, with anxious and woe...
Or ones with gardens of plenty - forever loved, meshed, pampered, adored...

THAT KINDA' LOVE...

Beryl Rayford

That kind you can't escape.
That kind you don't want to escape.
That kind you want to work on because it's successful love.
Love like breathing - necessary to exist. The pain is minor compared to the benefits.
That everyday getting on your nerves... yet, you depend on it to know everything is alright.
That kinda love.
That kind where you can't overlook, diminish, take for granted kind of love...
It shines too bright; or lies dormant...
There, below the surface, with that certainty of routine.
Obvious, but never easy...
So many attempts to understand... yet, it's understood - one can't be Without the other...
Yeah! That kinda love...
The yin and yang; black and white; can't understand it, but will surrender to experience it... Yeah...
That kinda love...

THAT KINDA' LOVE

Beryl Rayford

In Miami, when Cyrus first laid eyes on Winifred - better known as "Winnie" – he knew she was the One because of the way the bottom of his stomach trembled. He put down the suitcases he was carrying as part of his railroad job.

Cyrus admired the way she carried herself. He knew she was not average. He shyly approached the young woman because he was easily 20 years her senior. Upon speaking to her, he heard the melodic Bahamian accent and dreamt of what he missed.

The easy smile on his lips; the desire to deeply please and be pleased were revealed for all to see. He was not satisfied with his life and wanted more. And Winnie looked like *more* to Cyrus.

Winnie, on the other hand, was more practical in her assessment of Cyrus and his needs. As a widow, Winnie, though quite capable of taking care of herself and her son, knew additional financial resources would be helpful.

She had just migrated from Grand Bahamas and was looking to make a new life. In her eyes, Cyrus would be a good provider with his railroad job and make beautiful children.

Yes, she was vain, highly intelligent and had a life plan.

Both had become the answers to each other's deepest prayers.

After spending time courting, the couple married. They both worked hard building small businesses and loved just as hard. Cyrus cherished Winnie because of her sharp mind, willingness to work and have a family. Her natural beauty enthralled her husband.

Winnie was unaware of the kids, wife and goat farm Cyrus left in Georgia. After a couple of years, Cyrus' first wife had him arrested for bigamy. He served his time; promptly divorced his first wife and remarried Winnie.

Their love for one another lasted for the rest of their lives, producing three more children. In their later years, they held hands, rubbed each other affectionately and gazed at one another, knowing that love was enough.

That kinda love.

THAT KINDA' LOVE

Beryl Rayford

You know that self love.
When you know what you deserve.
When you are willing to go deeper to constantly discover your strength.
When you sacrifice frivolity for that which lasts.
That which brings you peace, light and serenity.
That self love that glows like spun golden sunshine that cannot be touched by mere instances or occurrences.
I love myself like nobody else can but God.
That kinda love.

WHAT KIND OF A WOMAN?

Kimberly Shelton

What kind of a woman would have an affair with a married man? A selfish one? A needy one? One who has no regard for the feelings of others? One who has no self-esteem? One who hasn't thought ahead as to the ramifications of her actions? One who is easy? One who is a slut, a marriage-breaker? One who doesn't care? One who only cares about herself and getting her needs met? One who craves attention and touch?

One who wants to be desired? One who doesn't realize at the time that she will be blamed and shamed? One who doesn't know how to say 'No', either for fear she will hurt his feelings or because she hasn't learned how to? One who feels she isn't deserving of his full presence in the relationship?

One who subconsciously self-sabotages? One who only wants a part-time lover? One who is unable to have an emotionally committed relationship? One who easily succumbs to sexual advances? Or is it one who, "just couldn't help it?"

Perhaps it's someone who feels trapped in her circumstances for financial reasons or "because of the kids."

Someone whose only desire was to have a fling? Or someone who wanted more than anything else in the world to be adored, cherished, loved unconditionally and accepted for who and what she was? Someone who was willing to sacrifice anything and everything to know what it would be like to feel that way, if only for a moment?

Or, is it someone who just wanted to taste forbidden fruit? Someone who only desired the erotic, the kinky, the kind of sex she would never have otherwise? Is it someone who was willing to let herself experience that with someone other than her partner?

Is it someone who feels safe for the mere fact that he is married and she thinks he will never leave his wife? Or is it someone who never sowed her wild oats?

Someone who was so deprived of physical touch, who had not had so much as a kiss for over a quarter of a century even though she was in a committed relationship? Or is it someone who was desperate and longed for physical touch of any kind from anywhere she could get it, no matter the source?

Is it someone who doesn't love herself? Doesn't know how to because she was never loved or valued as a child? Is it someone who would accept sex when what she *really* wants is to be loved? Is it someone who isn't honorable, who has no conscience, who could care less about anyone else but herself?

Is it someone who considers herself an honest person? One who would never do such a thing under ordinary circumstances? Or is it someone who feels she deserves to get her needs met no matter what the cost or who is hurt in the process? Is it someone who would feel guilt and shame if anyone found out? Or is it someone who would feel great remorse if it resulted in him getting a divorce?

Is it someone who secretly wishes he would leave his wife? Is it someone who swears she will never take him for granted like his wife does? Is it someone who wishes with all her heart that he was hers?

Perhaps, it is someone who doesn't think enough of herself to not do what she knows is wrong. Or, it is someone who wants what she wants and won't settle for anything less until she has it?

Is it someone who feels she's found her one true love in this lifetime? Or is it someone who feels his wife is the luckiest woman in the world?

I know all of this to be true because I am that someone.

THE CHOICE

Kimberly Shelton

Why does it have to come down to this? A decision must be made, one way or the other. It's my point of no return.

It was inevitable, I guess. I felt all along it would eventually become an issue and it has. A Big One! *The one*. As if nothing else we have built together matters. As to whether or not we will spend our lives together. As if it's the only thing of merit.

And, I am split in two. There is NO solution to this. No way to come to terms. No way to agree to disagree. No compromise to be had. The dye has been cast... there is no turning back.

So, why would I meet the love of my life only to have this become the deciding factor? Why is most everything else so right when this one thing is so very wrong? Why can't a meeting of the minds be had? An amicable solution that suits us both?

Is it, "his way or the highway?" Apparently so. The asphalt beckons.

Why would the Universe send me **the one** only to have this be the issue? The deal-breaker. The End.

When we first met I remember thinking, "he keeps doing everything right." I have waited my entire life for him and now this seems like a cruel joke. I don't understand why a compromise can't be made if only for a little while until my pets are gone.

Why do I have to choose between them or him? They are my kids. I can't... give up either of them – my pets or him. I love them both to the depths of my soul. My heart will break either way.

And so, yet again, I have found myself in a hopeless situation when it comes to love. The issue can't be resolved by wishing it away. By hoping it will be any different than what it is. It's either him or them and the price is higher than I am willing to pay.

And so, it's back to being alone...again...

HE SAID HE LOVED ME...

Kimberly Shelton

He said he loved me. I believed him.
That was the first of many mistakes I made.
Accepting the words at face value without looking at the actions behind them. Syrupy sweet, strategic ones, dripping with exaggerated professions of love for me. All intentionally orchestrated to do one thing and one thing only...

To strip me of my money, as much and as often as he possibly could, so he could indulge in his *true* love, crack cocaine. Meanwhile, robbing me of any vestige of self-esteem or dignity... leaving me with not a shred of either in the end.

Only an empty bank account, cascades of stinging, searing tears and a heart so broken I would never recover. His actions had purpose, pre-meditated, specifically designed to seduce... to manipulate, to surreptitiously pull my heartstrings so I would be compelled to open my heart and my wallet.

Never any intention of following through on his promises. Extortion, it's what he had in mind all along. I was only his latest victim. He garnered sympathy with fabricated lies. It worked. I believed him... only to be exploited, used, abused... My trust given so freely, my belief in his loaded, but empty words proved to be lethal to me.

Dangerous, a predator, a thief, a psychopath, a narcissist, an orchestrator of lies... It's who and what he is, a professional con artist specializing in preying on hopeful and lonely women. One who knows exactly what to say so they succumb to his wishes, one infinitely skilled in the art of coercion.

I didn't stand a chance. I was easy prey, a prime target, the trusting one... Didn't have a clue as to what I was up against. I was low-hanging fruit, an amateur unaware I was playing in a game with a professional, a trusting gullible woman who just wanted to be loved. One who wanted to believe that what he said was true. I chose to accept the sob story that is believable only to the naïve and uninitiated.

He stole from me, took what I didn't have to give... my hard-earned money and played upon my sympathy and empathy.

He used my compassion for his concocted plight to his advantage, deviously raping me on every level - mentally, emotionally, spiritually and physically.

He seized my heart, my hope, my trust...
He said he loved me. I believed him.

DATING AFTER 50

Kimberly Shelton

So, you think you want love? Think again... Especially if you are a woman in her 50s and beyond. The bitter truth is that men our age are looking for young women, women in their 30s, an arm charm, someone to have sex with that still looks halfway decent as if that were the only thing that matters.

Are you prepared to suffer the rejection that is inevitable when he:

Sees you without makeup? Isn't thrilled when you undress for the first time? Notices the inner tube around your middle? Scrutinizes the cellulite on your thighs, your varicose veins, the flabby skin that's lost its elasticity, the diminished collagen of your youth that's left nothing but lines and wrinkles, the gray hair that's not just on your head, discovers your multiple health issues?

And, what about things unseen? The stuff below the surface...your hurts, fears and traumas, your abandonment issues?

The things you're most embarrassed about, the stuff you'd prefer remained hidden, the secrets you don't want revealed?

And, those things only scratch the surface. Will he accepts you 'warts and all?'

That said, why would any of us even consider subjecting ourselves to such intense scrutiny or put ourselves in such a vulnerable position? Why are we willing to succumb to the mere possibility of rejection? Why would we allow ourselves to be so exposed?

Because to not do so means we are choosing to forgo the chance to love, to miss the very thing we want most in the world, which is to be loved. For all its perils, we have no choice but to risk it all, throw caution to the wind, to embrace the potential of excruciating pain in order to reach the heights of joy... to bask in the ecstasy of love.

And, it is for this that we risk... again and again...

THE COIN TOSS

Kimberly Shelton

I had no idea at the time that what I would find that day in the flowerbed would change my life forever. Her presence announced only by a wagging tail. The remainder of her body blended into the scenery and would've otherwise gone unnoticed.

She trailed my every move all day and when it came time for me to leave, I struggled with what to do. Should I take her with me or leave her here? Did she belong to someone and was lost? What would happen to her if I left her? What would my sister say if I showed up with another dog? Would my two dogs, Winston and Savannah, accept her?

The questions swirled, as I struggled with what to do. I decided to take her with the intention of trying to find her a good home.

The next day, I called the Humane Society and put her on a waiting list. They said they would call when a space became available and that I would have 24 hours to call them back. Every time they called, I was out of town and unable to return the call before the deadline. This was before cell phones.

After the third time, I became annoyed and called to let them know of my dissatisfaction with their policy and my inability to get her placed because of the missed calls. I explained my situation and demanded to be moved to the top of the list when they had an opening. They agreed to accept my call whenever I was able to pick up their message.

I hung up satisfied that she would be next on the list. I was convinced that having three dogs was too many, but I was also becoming attached to her and feeling more and more anxious about letting her go.

Another month went by and I received the phone call I had been waiting for for over a year. They were ready for her. When I heard the message on my answering machine, I was relieved but also divided. I had developed feelings for her. I struggled... should I keep her or let her go? It was agonizing, I could not decide!

At the time, I was reading a book titled, *Just Listen.* I flipped through the pages and discovered a chapter on how to make decisions. As I read the chapter, I said, "This is it!" I can finally decide. The book's instructions were to write down all the pros and cons of the dilemma, to close my eyes, take a deep breath and flip a coin. Heads, it's yes, I keep her; tails, it's no, I don't...

"Quick, do it, don't think!"

Then, I was to pay attention to my first thoughts as I registered the result of the coin toss, to notice my immediate, spontaneous reaction to the result. Was I relieved and happy? If so, this is my choice. Was I disappointed or sad? If so, go with the other choice. I was to trust my intuitive response, my gut.

So, I got quiet within myself, closed my eyes, took a deep breath and flipped the coin. I was a nervous wreck. I opened my eyes to see the verdict and breathed a huge sigh of relief.

It was heads! She gets to stay! I was elated to call the Humane Society the next day to tell them I would not be surrendering her... that I was in love.

They concurred. "That's what we like to hear!"

Unbeknownst to me, that random coin toss was the most pivotal point in my life, for she became my soulmate, my confidant, my everything. Never have I experienced such adoration, love and acceptance. The greatest gift of my life is what she was to me. She healed my broken heart and taught me to love again.

Looking back, I shudder to think just how close I came to never having experienced such a deep and profound love, how I would have missed out on the greatest love I have ever known had the coin toss been "tails."

The fate of her life rested in a coin toss. I thank God every day for that "heads up."

MY OREO

Kimberly Shelton

Yesterday, happiness abounded in her wagging tail and
                          sparkling, joyous eyes
Today, a resident in the emergency room, desperately fighting
               for her life
    Tomorrow, mere granules, returned to me in a small wooden box
         bearing only the inscription of who she used to be

What is it, exactly, that deems one moment fine and the next not?
        The instant when everything changes... becomes irreversible...
When yes turns to no, longing to despair, hope to hopelessness

So where does the love go now that she has ascended to the ethers?
         Does it remain in my heart alongside the memories?
Or does it dissipate with her absence?

      And what am I left with now that she's gone?
      Silence. Emptiness. A void that only she can fill...
      Our walks, our talks, our kisses, our cuddles...
           Just a memory as she is...
           Only reminiscence remains...

MY BEACH WEEK CRUSH

Elizabeth "Libby" Smoot

On my last first day of high school, I looked forward to one thing - Beach Week. My Girl Squad secured, along with my deposit, those June days that couldn't arrive fast enough.

Beach Week had come to its reputation honestly. Mention it decades later and heads nod in hazy tribute. Newly minted adults, running amok in packs, many without parental supervision for the first time in their lives.

Hot sun, hard bodies and parties that blended night into day...

That is, unless you stayed at 42nd Street in Ocean City, MD in 1979. There, four young ladies who craved only sun, sand and temporary freedom lived for a week in an upper-level beach house. The previous four years were spent hitting the books, courts and fields, we were teammates in need of respite before moving on to whatever called our names.

Things went according to plan for most of the week. We avoided the higher-numbered streets with classmates doing publicly what they had only done privately before. Not our scene. Forty-Second street was just what we ordered.

Lazy days, lazy nights...

And then on the last night, the scenery suddenly shifted when new neighbors moved in next door. Boys from a popular private Catholic school, mysterious and gorgeous....

What were four young women, now tanned and feeling a bit melancholy at our leaving, to do?

Accepting their party invite, we headed up those steep steps that evening in our satin jackets and white Nikes. I'm still not sure how I ended up walking on the beach with some nameless stranger.

High moon, humid air and angry waves...

Someone must have been looking out for me that evening. I suspect I disappointed that young man for a nanosecond and I suspect he remembers me not.

Still, those few short hours stayed with me. My Beach Week Crush.

A memory that gets my head to nodding when those poignant days come to mind.

LAUNCH

Elizabeth "Libby" Smoot

It was 4 p.m. when I noticed my oldest child trying to discreetly usher us out of her dorm room, a room she had occupied less than three hours had quickly become as comfortable as the "blankie" she once toted everywhere. That blankie, I noticed, was now tucked away on her new bed, outfitted with a new comforter and pillow for the new life that awaited.

We packed the car that morning, drove two hours and jockeyed for a parking space outside the four-story brick building she would call home for the next nine months – a structure that became my mortal enemy. After a dizzying array of trips between the car and her room, we unloaded all the possessions she found precious enough to keep. I was not one of them.

All the work to get to this day came flooding back: the never-ending parade of projects and ballgames, clubs and awards. She had arrived at this school, her top pick, her dream come true. We had prepared her for this moment, but I had forgotten to prepare myself.

Headed home, tears kept me company for many miles, but my heart never did catch up. Twenty years later, a piece of me still resides in that 16-foot by 12-foot cinder block room.

We laugh about that day now. The black and blue marks, the frantic run to a department store for supplies we forgot and her eagerness to bid the remnants of our family goodbye. It's just the way you want life to play out for your child – an independence springing forth. An eagerness to step outside familiar comfort zones and embrace what this new journey has to offer.

Oh, what it had to offer! A life I've been able to share in many ways, that lifts my spirits every time I hear her say, "Guess what happened today?"

She's no longer that little girl lugging around that pink blanket, but I remain the same Mama whose heart breaks every time she comes and goes. Only now, she's the one who wants to linger a little longer.

ARMOR AND APRON

Elizabeth "Libby" Smoot

We took our children on a beach vacation only once. I thought it would be relaxing, but they found the sand too itchy, the sun too hot and I worried all day about waves taking them out to sea. Something meant for good turned out so unexpectedly difficult.

Parenting can be the same. I hold onto precious memories of raising my children like our vacation sand castles, facing time and tide. With every encroaching wave, I feel those years slipping away from my memory.

Creating holiday traditions they could hold onto, endless dinners for baseball warriors, night after night reading favorite storybooks as they reached for slumber. I binge on those moments like a Netflix special, only to have them tease me as they fade to black.

If I didn't have the pictures, would I even be sure it all happened?

Cruelty, I have learned, exists to puncture a mother's heart. It hovers overhead like a black cloud, waiting silently and patiently until it finds the perfect moment to strike. A violent blow without apology.

Despite the pain of this part of my journey, had I known the heartache that awaited me in their leaving, nothing would have kept me from hearing those sweet voices call me "Mama." Could a sorority of mothers who preceded me have warned about the inevitable and interminable stretch of lonely days? Maybe, but it wouldn't have mattered. I would have simply said, "I'll do it better" and stepped into the arena with my armor. And, my apron...

Love is rooted in the abundant sacrificial acts between mother and child. It's a playing out of God's story in its purest form. We're designed to love, to be in a relationship, to commit to seeking the best for one another, despite the story's ending.

I treasure my chapter in the book, knowing my deepest joys and painful wounds live there. I loved it and it mattered, even though my heart feels as if it's eroding like those sand castles. Bit by bit.

JUST A SWINGIN'

Elizabeth "Libby" Smoot

One of life's razor thin choices
Greets me at the ole' ballyard
First base under the bright lights
Charlotte Johnson on the radio
There you stand, handsome and tall
Lifting your blue eyes to mine
Those eyes, those eyes, oh how they see me
Love at first sight.

Hearts captivated, promises pledged
Two lives made one at the altar
Conquering life's fast balls and curves
Blessings, joys; too much shared sorrow,
Our fairytale story slowly fading
On the first porch just a swingin'
Old eyes, old eyes, oh how they pierce me
Love in the dimming night.

AGAPE

Elizabeth "Libby" Smoot

Who am I to ponder the meaning of love? Poets, philosophers, songwriters through the ages have opined about this four-letter word with deeper contemplation than me and, yet, we continue to ask what it all means.

Four letters – taking up so much little space on a page, but one of the most examined subjects of all time.

For all the soul-searching and hand-wringing, it's quite simple, really. We love because God first loved us, St. John tell us. When we come to know love's Creator, we are welcomed into a relationship powered by this pure, unconditional virtue.

Some days, I am overwhelmed by the thought that I've never really loved at all. Not the way we're called to. With a selflessness that requires nothing in return. That seeks no measure of acknowledgement or appreciation.

This charitable love that the Greco-Christians found needed its own name – agape – is the highest form of love and the hardest of the loves to lavish on another. To love one's enemy. To be generous of spirit no matter the cost. To seek only another's best.

Can our fallible, human soul love without any interest in personal gain? Mother Teresa, agape's greatest example, is said to have felt like the greediest person alive because she derived a feeling of kindness from giving. If we can't count her as genuine, then who makes the list?

In his first century letter to the church at Corinth, St. Paul writes that love is patient and kind, not irritable and envious. Could it be Paul gave us this impossible list to show us that we can only love with agape by loving Christ who then loves through us?

Christ calls us to take up our cross and follow him – the very essence of agape that Paul writes about. To do that is to open one's heart to vulnerability, but also to experience life at is fullest.

To live and not just be alive.

A PRAYER FOR MY HEART

Trish Stukbauer

Father God,
I entrust to you my heart, battered and battle-weary as it is.
Teach it to love You first, so that it may, in turn, love others
as You do.
When it's ready, give it to someone who is worthy of it in your eyes.
No matter how it flutters, keep it away from those who would use it,
abuse its generosity, and lead it away from your plans.
Give it to someone who will treasure it, nurture it, trust it and challenge it,
someone who will love that my heart does the same for his.
In Jesus' name, I pray.
Amen.

UNPRINTABLE

Trish Stukbauer

Writers bare their souls, yet some emotions are best left cloaked.
Words that would curl the pages they'd grace.
Raw emotions lay naked; exposed to impotent scrutiny.
Change the names, the time, the details, the place.

No matter.
Secret thoughts clear to those who think they know...
Nothing is sacrosanct – not age, race, status...
Boundaries erased.

Hearts don't care about lines drawn in societal sand,
Even as souls wrestle against undisciplined desires.
Try to mask them as you will.
Truth still scorches.

"TO MY GOD-DAMN YANKEE"

Trish Stukbauer

She meticulously etched those words into a silver prayer card case with a pocket knife.
No engraving shops were open as The Blitz screamed above Sheffield's skies.
Lives cut short on streets that never should have seen blood.
Somehow, in the midst of war, they found each other.
An "overpaid, oversexed and over here" engineer who labored on airplane engines behind the lines,
wracked with guilt because his older brother was killed in action in Market Garden,
sought comfort in the arms of a true British beauty with a cocky attitude.
Surrender and a brother's miraculous return should have ended a delightfully distracting dalliance.
No, she crossed the ocean to be with him.
And he bridged prejudice to be with her.
A shining star, brighter than the lights of LA he moved her to.
That fire blazed for 30 years until cancer tore apart a love that withstood war and peace
and haunted the final decades of his life; he was without his flower.

"With all my Love, Lily"

Red Birds & Roses

Trish Stukbauer

Signs are everywhere, if we look for them.

When Matt left this earth, far too young
I saw his guiding hand in every sunset sky trail
and heard his echo in all too familiar songs.

When mom left this earth, far too fast
I saw her spirit in every cardinal that flew
at day's dawning and stopped to perch
just outside my window until tears fell.

When love left my life, far too violently
I remembered every rose
and felt every thorn, cutting
until there was no blood left to give.

Over the long nights, something changed.
The sky trails blazed new paths.
The birds brought comfort with scarlet songs.
The roses blossomed in different shades.

Out of ashes, some things entered.
Strength to fly, comfort to give,
Courage to love again.

Signs are everywhere, when we look for them.

LONGING

Trish Stukbauer

Just a fragment of a picture that would have yellowed if it resided on paper.
Chiseled abs that taper seductively into deliciously masculine hips.

Just a glimpse into what could have been; should be now.
Tortured nights, sleeplessly dreaming of exploring well-muscled lines.

Just a moment that hasn't materialized;
Lived only in drenched imagination.

Just a chance touch, electricity pulsating through willing skin...
Confused by heightened emotions felt in isolation.

Just a thought that remains hidden;
Guarded hearts won't open.

Just a glance, revealing souls' longing for more than the physical...
Both remain out of reach.

WHERE ARE THE MEN?

Trish Stukbauer

I used to see them on my morning commute back when we still had one.

Thirty-somethings with man-buns carrying kids' backpacks on electric scooters.

The type of boys the other boys used to beat up. The ones the girls had to protect.

Maternal instincts kicking in at 10 as I stepped between a pack of bullies and a freckle-faced nerd.

Now, they are all grown up.

Emasculated by the continuing media drumbeat of "toxic masculinity."

Indoctrinated by a society that says being what we used to call a "real man" is a bad thing.

So why are women surprised when concepts like honor and integrity and fidelity are scarce?

When they run from a fight instead of leading the charge?

When they spurn real women for the arms of girls who check off key fobs and watch brands with a casual disregard for their hearts and souls?

When easy sex is just that, why should they bother chasing the real?

When we tell them to back down, should we be surprised when they don't stand up?

When we tear them down, should we be shocked that they can't rise?

When we allow our boys to be muzzled, should we be surprised that they grow into men without a voice?

So, before we ask, where are the real men? We should ask if we are woman enough to stand by their side.

TO LOVE IS DIVINE

Diane Weekley

Love is a decision. Love is grueling. Love is impatient. Love is unkind.
Love keeps account of wrongs. Love defines us. Love maligns us.
Love abandons us.
To love is divine.
Love is patient. Love is kind. Loves does not keep account of wrongs.
Love accepts all things. Love tolerates all things. Love endures through great pain.
To love is divine.
Love is a bond that cannot be broken under a tsunami of experience and emotion. Love endures. Love circles back like a hawk targeting its prey.
To love is divine.
Love is chemistry. Love is pheromones. Love is a tidal wave of emotion. Love is energy in motion. Love extracts our best selves. Love extrudes our worst selves.
To love is divine.
This thing called Love confuses, calls, conjoins. Gives, takes, survives. Disguised in friendship, cloaked in right action. Hidden between the lines.
To love is divine.
Love gives Life. Love takes away. Broadcast the blueprint. Mail the map. Dispatch the design.
I am waiting.
Send the Divine.

FATHER, LOVER, UNCLE, BROTHER

Diane Weekley

Father, Lover,
Uncle, Brother
Such a way to see. Looking for a man to fly,
Fly away with me.

Mystic turning cyclic tide,
Seer of old songs. Hunting for his youth he cries,
thinking not of wrongs.

You can make the Sun to rise
You can soothe my eyes. You can veil the mist so high
You can sail my thighs.

Wrapped together, mysterious tether
Break the chain, relieve the plain.
Heal hurt, dissolve into rain.

Embrace love's measure
Begin anew.

ELECTRIC LOVE

Diane Weekley

The day Himeros lived, agent of divine power, transformed into a human body, intense, alive... A mere touch, a lingering glance, shattered mundane reality and electrified my experience. It was a day when anything and everything enchanted, energized, erupted safe havens...

A friend, a fellow theater major, came to me with an ask. Her brother was in town. Would I meet him? Spend the day with him? He's a bit different. I think you'd get on.

We met.

In my memory, he is tall, rugged, muscular and wide brown eyes that took in every nano-bite. Warm, beckoning, welcoming... Ebony hair, wild, tumbling over his ears, blown away from a face like a fairy, slightly mischievous, innocently poised for entrapment.

Time obscures details and accurate retelling, but never truth. Only his essence remains.

The energy field within, around him, engulfed like a tidal wave, accelerated and pinged every particle, infused every cell. I felt as if no one else had ever known me like he knew me. Being with him was like a Vulcan mind meld, invasive, seductive, violent...

I remember running across fields, hand in hand, as if lifted by the wind. At the bottom of the hill, we stood breathless, laughing... His touch, pure, gentle, crossed every line, melted every wall.

We kissed.

My universe exploded. Like air raid sirens during The Blitz, every instinct for self-preservation and survival came online. He invited us to find a secluded place, beckoned with a tender touch. This was no small fire, but a torch that would consume and obliterate. Sex would be the end of me.

I said No. He imploded, his light darkened, energy shrank... the conducting pathway disappeared.

He left.

Two weeks later, he was dead. Suicide. His life force misplaced in a shell too vulnerable to withstand this reality, vanished into *his* safety.

I wondered if I had said Yes, would he have found refuge even for a moment and not chosen oblivion?

It was Him or Me.

LET'S LOVE LIKE CATS AND DOGS

Diane Weekley

Dogs and cats are supposed to fight like cats and dogs.

But not Lacie and Bingo. They were an unlikely pairing. Bingo showed up the day I lay on the living room couch, too sick to say no to my young sons' pleas. A beautiful black Labrador-Shepherd mix, able to swivel mid-air like a weathervane spun by a gust of wind, he romped through our yard.

No doubt abandoned based on his ribcage, needing a home and a family. Too exhausted to refute their persuasive arguments, I said yes.

We'd have to put up signs and try to find the owner, but yes. Love at first sight. I didn't know that. Not until I burst into tears when given the choice to treat Bingo's heartworms with a regimen of shots and medicine culminating in a $700 vet stay, or let it go and allow the dog to die.

No brainer. Find the funds. That's what love does.

Lacie came later. Predisposed not to like cats since my college roommate's cat defecated behind our stand-alone stove, I did not want to say yes to Lacie. Cats mean cat hair and require constant litter box cleaning to restrict ammonia smells. Cat claws shred curtains and upholstery.

Lacie started out as an outside cat where she belonged. Bingo and Lacie's détente lingered, laden with hisses and growls. Gradually, outdoors became indoors. Overtime, an uncommon friendship evolved, culminating in daily naps together on the dog pad, nested like spoons in a drawer.

One day after the usual great escape to do neighborhood reconnaissance, Bingo loped toward the house and crumbled at the foot of the mailbox. His heart gave out. Our hearts broke. My oldest son delayed work to help bury him in our future backyard pet cemetery.

We shared love stories. Beautiful, loyal, loving Bingo stories.

No one noticed Lacie, didn't think too much about her. For a day or two, she padded from room to room, meowing and unsettled. One day Lacie meowed to go out. We watched as she prowled toward the grave, sat, face forward, statue still.

Minutes became an hour.

Graveside visitations continued daily that summer. Her best friend lay buried beneath dirt and rocks. The house felt empty. Less and less did she lay on the dog pad. We put it away and invited her to the couch.

Lacie became a powerful reminder of the power of love and friendship.

Lacie now rests next to Bingo under flagstone.

THIS THING CALLED LOVE

Diane Weekley

I struggle with this thing called love, this 'crazy little thing called love.' Can you hear it? Queen or Dwight Yoakam singing? That's my soundtrack.

You'd think at 60 something I should know the score.

What is love anyway? What is loving? What is the right way to love? Is there a right way? What is too much love? What is constricting love, co-dependent love, true love? What is how do we love?

You'd think I should have figured it out by now.

What is supportive love, family love? This thing called love, so hard to know what is real, growing up in an alcoholic home where love butts up against 'I told you so' moments of blissful embrace and blatant neglect fueled by Smirnoff, Tom Collins and bourbon highballs.

Was it loving to laugh at my little brother, three years old, toddling around the coffee table strewn with half-empty whiskey cocktail glasses, deftly draining them one at a time? Down the hatch!

Was it loving to come begging for safety from my mother to protect against the little boy who tried to trap me in a closet to fiddle me at age six and have my mother tell me it's all in my head? Too caught up in coffee klatch conversation over cocktails to pay attention.

To find my way out, I explored AA, Al-Anon, Codependent No More titles and other recovery pathways.

Love is boundaries, loyalty, acts of kindness. Love is respect, tolerance, attention. Love is heat, chill, Netflix & Chill. Love is listening when you think there is nothing left to give, silence when you want to defend, compassion in place of condemnation.

For self and others, I do believe there "is no greater love than laying down one's life for a friend." It starts with befriending oneself.

That is the beginning of understanding "this thing called love."

LETTERS TO SELF

Dearest Lizz:

When life's winding roads separate us. Be reminded of what I love most. You are electric. Bottled sunshine bursting, inextinguishable... You glow and embody sexy, brilliant light appropriate for any affair. Invisible magnetic forces call for more of your Energy. Vibration. Love. It is who you are. Keep shining.

Yours always,
Elizabeth Anne

Dear Me:

Let go of the fear of disappointment, the fear of embarrassment, the fear of failure and embrace the fullness of life. In the words of Les Brown, "Live full, die empty." Life isn't going to go your way. You have to go your way and take life with you! You have to demonstrate a willingness to patiently persevere, which will lead you to the best version of yourself – one where your character is in alignment with God's.

Ty Burton

Note to Self:

(Apologies for the length of my letter. At my age, who follows directions?)

At this stage of my life, there is so much I can say. I am pleased with my journey, having endured the challenges and realities. One of my favorite elements is that I - though very late in life - finally stopped telling Jesus, "No!" That changed the path. I finally saw that God's grace was with me all along even when life, death and danger presented itself.

Although the "stupid monster" still tried to take me down and stop my forward motion, I chose to laugh at failure and get back up. That qualifies me as a daughter of the Most High God, above no one, below no one.

I finally saw my value, having been thrown opportunities (my favorite word). And best of all, I find myself in HIS purpose for life. Yea! Well done!

Now, as I turn the page to 80 years on Earth, I have a voice, so I must let it rip. Pour it onto the page and use past pain to encourage others to stay the course. Use the joy I have discovered to hug hurting hearts and speak words that lift.

There is work to be done, Toni. There are opportunities and people I can bless. Go for it! My past is over, my present is unlimited as long as I have breath and I have a future full of next steps. When I put my head on the pillow at night, there is peace in my soul.

Toni

Dear Lori (Davis),

You are loved more than you could ever know! At times, you were a scared little girl hiding behind your Grandmother's legs. At times, you felt adored looking into the eyes of a lover. What a journey this life has been so far! The ups and downs have molded you into the strong, loving, caring woman you are today. Get Ready! There is so much more coming your way!

Hey Love:

I know you don't believe I'm here for you. Realize it, I am. Know that in the worst of moments, I hold you close, healing your fumbled heart. In the scariest of darkness, I touch your cheek and tell you how amazing you are. In the best of times, we dance!

Doreen

Hey Buddy:

Let's go for a walk. See that sun. Let go now. It's gone. Bothers you none. In fact, it's all one big symphony composed for; without, and through you, so saying 'I love you' means everything. So, too, smiling, laughing and caring earnestly.

Love,
JB

P.S. Here's looking at you.

Letter to Self:

I'm writing this to you in the future, as I am much older and want to reminisce about the past. We've come a long way from a shy and insecure young girl to a confident powerhouse businesswoman. It took determination, grit and self-belief. You did it! It is now time to celebrate the successes and look at the failures as building blocks that made you the extraordinary woman you are today.

Love Alice

Dear Self:

You entered this world with wide-eyed curiosity, incessant WHY questions, an imagination you could be anything and a 'conquer the world' attitude. Detours dampened that spirit at times, but you overcame life's obstacles and persevered. Continue living your joyous blessed life, filled with love and always 'lift as you soar."

Lori (Myers)

Dear Marisa:

Shakespeare wrote, "Though she be but little, she is fierce." Add tenacious, resilient and strong. You are a *Parrhesiastes*. You have a passion for words and a need to fix what is broken. This is the blood that fuels your heart. Thump, Thump, Thump, Thump, Thump, Thump... Do yourself a favor. Stop fighting against the tide.

M

Dear Proctor:

What a %*&%&! trip this life has been? Thankful that I'm still here - raising hell, hiding little, still grinding, loving those that care and support, hoping to play basketball again, write more poetry, finish my **list** and coach more folks before the Good Brother upstairs takes me away. To survive, believe in the face in the mirror. With many blessings, I've traveled my own crazy - hustled, learned, loved, won and lost; always with sharp edges in my mind and my pocket."

Gunny

Hey Beryl:

I love you, girl! No matter what life throws your way, you handle it. You may make mistakes, but nobody really knows what they are doing in life, so live and love fully. You are the most important person, except God. Get it chick!

Love you always.

My Dearest Kimberly:

Since the beginning, you've had a difficult life. From being an "accident," to enduring the abusiveness of your father that catapulted you into a world of humiliation and despondency, it's been a tough road. But, thanks to years of therapy, you're well on your way to a much better future. You're not broken beyond repair as you've always believed. You have overcome your malicious childhood. You're turning your wounds into stepping stones.

Dear Self:

If I could have removed your pain, I would have. I would have kept it from searing your memory because you're loved by the only one who matters. You knew it. It just took you awhile to figure it out. Now go. Press on. Spread the love.

Libby Smoot

Dear Me:

You have grown so much from that wide-eyed, over-protected girl who thought life would be a fairytale. Along the way, you shed the glass slippers and became a knight, standing against evil and mediocrity. Now, loving the face in the cracked mirror with an open heart that will not settle.

T

Hey there, Didi,

Keep believing, keep going. Stay green and growing. Live with courage, creativity and generosity. There is no other person on this Earth like you; no one called to your specific purpose. Live joyously. Listen to your internal compass. Use your senses. Live out loud.

Ciao bella,
Diane

BOOKS BY OUR WRITERS (available amazon.com)

* Ty Burton
    A JOURNEY TO MANHOOD: The Village That Raised The Boy
* Toni Cordell
    PUPPY BY THE SIDE OF THE ROAD
* Lori Ann Davis
    UNMASKING SECRETS TO UNSTOPPABLE RELATIONSHIPS

    LOVE HABITS Easy Strategies for a Stronger Happier Relationship

    A COUPLE'S LOVE JOURNAL 52 Weeks to Reignite Your Relationship, Deepen Communication and Strengthen Your Bond

    RADICAL SELF LOVE (Lori Ann Davis and Laura Menze)

    365 WAYS TO IGNITE HER LOVE (Chris Reshetar and Lori Ann Davis)

    READY, SET, DATE By 12 Leading Dating Experts
* Lori Myers
    GLIMPSES OF TENDERNESS Soothing the Soul Through Reminiscence
* Glenn Proctor
    750 QUESTIONS Worth Asking Yourself or Your Significant Other tweets, greets, sweets & beets A GUIDE TO MANAGING EGO (e-book)

    Finding Dust Trilogy
    - **KICKING BOTTLES, NEWS & DUST** An Autobiography – 50 Years of Poems
    - **Love, Lust & Flirts**
    - **CHANGE Robots Driving Covered Wagons**
* Trish Stukbauer,
    - **REMODELING and NEW CONSTRUCTION with NO REGRETS** (with Gary and Pam Palmer)
    - **There is a Moth in Daddy's Coffee (by Michael Desroches, edited by Trish)**
    - **Make it a Great Day** (with Henry Donaghy)

COMING SOON:
* Lizz Baxter
    ARMY GIRL Stories of Womanhood in Combat Boots